Achieving Positive Outcomes for Children in Care

A Lucky Duck Book

Achieving Positive Outcomes for Children in Care

R.J. (Seán) Cameron and
Colin Maginn

⑤SAGE

Los Angeles | London | New Delhi
Singapore | Washington DC

First published 2009
Reprinted 2009

SAGE Publications
1 Oliver's Yard
55 City road
London EC1Y 1SP

SAGE Publications Inc.
2455 Teller Road
Thousand Oaks, California 91320

SAGE Publications India Pvt Ltd
B 1/I 1 Mohan Cooperative Industrial Area
Mathura Road, New Delhi 110 044

SAGE Publications Asia-Pacific Pte Ltd
33 Pekin Street #02-01
Far East Square
Singapore 048763

Library of Congress Control Number: 2009929032

British Library Cataloguing in Publication data

A catalogue record for this book is available from the British Library

ISBN 978-1-84787-448-1
ISBN 978-1-84787-449-8 (pbk)

Typeset by C&M Digitals (P) Ltd, Chennai, India
Printed by MPG Books Group, Bodmin, Cornwall
Printed on paper from sustainable resources

To our parents

Contents

Preface

Why we have written this book...

I and the public know
What all school children learn,
Those to whom evil is done
Do evil in return.

(W.H. Auden, 1907–73)

Tracey was nine but she looked much younger. The tirade of insulting words, punches, kicks and attempts to bite Carole, the senior carer on duty, was recorded as 'yet another temper tantrum'. This was the fourth tantrum that day and it was only lunchtime. Tracey had recently been admitted to our children's home and as the director, I had met her several times and she always seemed anxious, angry and preoccupied.

This was the early days of the Pillars of Parenting and Tracey was one of the first children to benefit from the approach. Using the methods and theories described in this book, the consultant psychologist had worked with the staff of the children's home to identify Tracey's parenting needs, agree strategies to respond to her pain-based behaviour and to identify and begin to build on her strengths.

About six weeks after we started her carefully worked out support plan, I was sharing a drink and a biscuit with members of staff and a little group of our children when Tracey came bouncing into the kitchen singing: she stopped, looked at me and to the surprise of everyone, she asked 'Who are you?'

By then, Tracey's temper tantrums had almost disappeared.She had progressed from defensive, fear-induced anger to beginning to trust adults again, to feel safeand to explore her surroundings. Six weeks earlier, her world view had been constricted by fear, in her frightened and angry state, she could see no further than her immediate perceived needs. Now having experienced the right kind of support from the staff, she felt safe enough to explore, and it was in this expanded world that she saw me for the first time.

Although seeing Tracey's new-found joy and pleasure with life still fills me with pride, we won't mention her again, but this book was written for her and the many traumatised children like her. The approach described in the following pages calls for clarity of roles for the many people caring for looked-after children. It sets out to empower those working with the children on a 24/7 basis, with the knowledge and skills to understand the complexity of their task. Our 'Authentic Warmth' model of childcare requires clear and strong leadership from those responsible for organising services to children in public care and demands a high level of purposeful kindness and commitment from the carers who look after them every day. Most of all, it calls for a child-centred approach that is informed by the best knowledge 'psychology' has to offer.

Colin Maginn and R.J. (Seán) Cameron   April 2009

List of Figures and Tables

Figures

Tables

About the Authors

Dr R.J. (Seán) Cameron is founder and now Co-Director of the Professional Doctorate in Educational Psychology at University College London. He is also a private consultant in child and educational psychology.

His publication record is considerable, having written or edited five books and published more than 50 journal articles on a variety of topics including the management of behaviour at home and school, promoting organisational change in schools, working with the parents of young children who have severe developmental delay, and supporting residential and foster carers responsible for vulnerable children and young people.

In 2004 he was given the British Psychological Society's national award for distinguished contributions to the teaching of psychology.

Colin Maginn has worked with looked-after children in a variety of settings, including two separate secure units. Colin has a passion for excellence in childcare and is on a mission to improve the lives of vulnerable children and young people!

He believes that this important life-changing work is undervalued and is working to transform both how carers are viewed and what they do. To achieve this, working with Seán Cameron, they have developed a new model of professional childcare and have formed a social enterprise to work with foster carers and residential care staff. The approach is based on the concept of 'Authentic Warmth' and involves supporting and teaching carers to provide a highly sophisticated type of professional parenting, which meets the psychological needs of children who have been rejected, neglected and abused, and which also provides support for the young people's emotional adaptation.

Acknowledgements

Both authors would like to acknowledge, with sincere thanks, the important contributions of the residential care staff from the two London children's homes in which the 'Authentic Warmth' model of professional childcare was first developed.

The encouragement and support of Katie Metzler, commissioning editor at SAGE and Barbara Maines, project consultant, are also gratefully acknowledged.

1
Professional Childcare: When?

The supreme happiness of life is the conviction that we are loved.
(Victor Hugo, French novelist, 1802–85)

What makes a child carer a *professional*? Is it that they possess specialist knowledge and skills? Or is it just the fact that they are paid to look after other people's children? Our motivation for writing this book stems from our vision that, some day, the answer to this question will be an emphatic statement that includes the words 'a highly specialised knowledge of children's developmental needs, combined with effective therapeutic skills'. To reach this point in professional development, we would have to ensure that the knowledge and skills of carers can be effective, evidence based, flexible, dynamic (as opposed to static), drawing heavily on the knowledge-base of psychology, and not intimidated by our risk-averse legal system or frozen by political correctness.

There is still a long way to go to 'professionalise' childcare, not the least because almost everyone believes that they are experts in childcare. We have all been children and we have all retained the detailed and intimate knowledge of our own childhood. We know what we liked and disliked about the way we were brought up and, as individuals, we are well aware of what we think worked for us and we can vividly recall what did not. In retrospect, we can see how we spent our childhood years in building our view of the world and absorbing the norms of our culture. So, almost all of our own parenting styles, strategies and beliefs stem from our personal experiences of how we were brought up. Because these experiences were so powerful, most of us feel that we are general *experts in* parenting, rather than individuals who have been *recipients of* a specific parenting process.

As if universal 'expertosis' was not a big enough obstacle to a professional approach to childcare, few other professions have to surmount the claim that the skills which underpin it are 'instinctive'. Since we are part of the animal kingdom, where parenting is considered a natural and almost universal phenomenon, then what we do not already know (or have experienced during our own childhood) can be supplemented by instinct. If this is the case, surely the raising of other people's children should be a relatively straightforward task?

So what is the problem with this 'innate-plus-acquired' parenting skills' theory? After all, our close relatives, the gentle gorillas, mostly seem to be doing a competent job raising their offspring: they have no need for parenting books and gorilla children's homes are unheard off. The adult male silverback frequently takes on the parenting role when weaned gorillas are orphaned. Similarly, the reed warbler's dedicated care of its eggs is so strong that it can be ruthlessly exploited by the cuckoo which seizes an unguarded moment to deposit her egg in the reed warbler's nest, so that the emerging cuckoo chick will be brought up by a first-rate stepmother. Indeed, the natural world has other fascinating examples of 'substitute carers' which are interesting because they are exceptional: the most likely outcome for abandoned offspring in the natural world is that they end up as the meal of a predator or meet some other untimely end.

Children in Public Care

Over the ages, specific human societies have developed sets of moral codes and legal obligations that have at their core the protection of the vulnerable youngster. Yet in terms of human evolution it is only relatively recently, with the Poor Law of 1563, that poor children in Britain were formally recognised as being in need of state support at all. Indeed, in his book *The Invention of Childhood*, Cunningham (2006) observed that in the history of childhood we are constantly confronted with parents trying to cope with the deaths of their children, and children facing the possibility of their own deaths. It was not until the advent of eighteenth-century industrial Britain that child mortality rates began to drop. Before this, children died in large numbers from disease, malnutrition, negligence and abuse, or depended on the 'poor house' or the philanthropy of the community or the church.

While we in Britain are currently enjoying a society which directs considerable resources towards the needs of our children, these sobering historical facts are an important reminder that we should not underestimate the primary needs of children, that is, basic health care and food. But what else do successful residential or foster carers have to do to ensure that the children and young people they look after become healthy and happy adults who go on to succeed in relationships, provide a loving home for their own children, and lead fulfilling and independent adult lives?

For those children who have been abused, neglected and rejected and who have been removed into public care, the outcome of what is meant to be a benign act by society often turn out to be disappointing, disheartening or despairing. Jackson and McParlin provide a sobering summary:

> Children who grow up in local authority care, 'looked after' under the Children Act 1989, are four times more likely than others to require the help of mental health services; nine times more likely to have special needs

Table 1.1 Government initiatives to improve the quality of life for children and young people in care

- **Quality Protects.** In September 1998 the government launched 'Quality protects' At that time, the Secretary of State for Health, Frank Dobson, introduced the idea of 'corporate parents' when, addressing local authority councillors, he suggested that they should ask themselves 'Is this good enough for my child?' 'Quality protects' funding was provided to local authorities, based on targets set by the government, which aimed at improving outcomes for looked-after children. Improving educational outcomes was a top priority
- **Every Child Matters.** Following the death of Victoria Climbié, and the subsequent Inquiry by Lord Laming, in September 2003 the government launched their 'Every Child Matters' initiative, which set out five key outcomes or goals for every child. These are: being healthy; staying safe; enjoying and achieving; making a positive contribution; and achieving economic well-being. Looked-after children were targeted for special help and local authorities were viewed as needing help and guidance on how they placed children in need. Out of this paper came the central government paper 'Choice protects' which specifically set out to increase the number of foster placements for looked-after children
- **Care Matters.** In October 2006 the Green Paper *Care Matters: Transforming the Lives of Children and Young People in Care* opened with an acknowledgement from the Secretary of State for Education and Skills, Alan Johnson, that 'The life chances of all children have improved but those of children in care have not improved at the same rate. The result is that children in care are now at greater risk of being left behind than was the case a few years ago – the gap has actually grown'. The subsequent White Paper, '*Care Matters: Time for Change*' in June 2007, shows a determination to improve the quality of life for children in care and reiterates many of the concerns which had already been identified in 'Quality protects', including the importance of education

requiring assessment, support or therapy; seven times more likely to misuse alcohol or drugs; 50 times more likely to wind up in prison; 60 times more likely to become homeless; and 66 times more likely to have children needing public care. (Jackson and McParlin, 2006, p. 90)

Given the amount of specifically targeted funding for looked-after children by UK central government initiatives such as 'Quality protects' (DfES, 2000) 'Choice protects' (DfES, 2003), Children's Workforce Strategy and 'Every Child Matters: change for children in social care' (DfES, 2005a; 2005b) it would seem unlikely that all the failings of the care system, highlighted above, are mainly resource related or due to political apathy. (See Table 1.1 for a summary of some of recent and major central government initiatives.)

What is particularly poignant about children and young people in public care is that, unlike the common, media-fuelled perception of these children and young people belonging to 'hoodie' gangs, subject to anti-social behaviour orders and who 'terrorising' communities, the majority of children who are taken into care are there through no fault of their own. The Office for National Statistics (2005) found that the reasons for placement were: abuse and neglect (42 per cent), family dysfunction (13 per cent), intense family stress (12 per cent), parental illness (7 per cent) and socially unacceptable behaviour (6 per cent). The figures

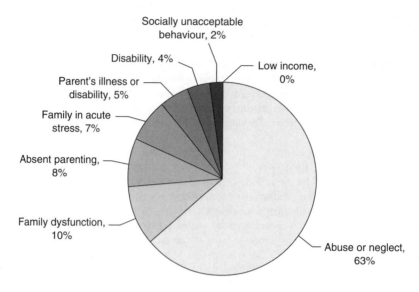

Figure 1.1 Children in care at 31 March 2005 by category of need

produced in the DfES (2006) publication *Care Matters: Transforming the Lives of Children and Young People in Care* rated the 'socially unacceptable behaviour' group as 2 per cent of the total (see the pie chart in Figure 1.1).

Returning to our vision of specialist knowledge and skills in professional childcare, according to the Children's Workforce Development Council (2008) there are about 170,000 adults responsible for the care of the 60,000-plus children and young people in public care. Given the poor outcomes and the clear pointers from the work of Jackson and McParlin (2006) an obvious conclusion is that this large group of professional carers has been let down by the insights from their own childhood, their culture and their parenting instincts; however, closer examination reveals a more complex explanation.

From Conflicting Views to Shared Purpose

The development of the 'Authentic Warmth' model of childcare described in this book, began in 2003 with a heated professional disagreement between the two authors, when Colin Maginn who was the director of two London children's homes and Seán Cameron, a child and educational psychologist working at University College London, embarked on an applied research project.

Colin had strongly disagreed with one of the conclusions in a published article on enhancing resilience in looked-after children (Dent and Cameron, 2003).

Their contention was that as well as the long-recognised risk factors in the lives of these children (such as illness and disease, economic adversity, exposure to violence, living in a drug and crime context, social and emotional deprivation, maltreatment at the hands of adults and other children, poor parenting and so on) a further factor could now be added to this risk list – being in public care. Colin's view was that a conscientious social worker or placement officer, could be influenced by such a conclusion and use it to avoid exposing children to such 'further risks' and decide to leave children who are at risk, with abusive, neglectful and rejecting parents. This is a concern, which has since been expressed in the 2008 the Welsh Assembly's review of the impact of care on children's welfare (Forrester et al., 2008).

Dent and Cameron's uncompromising statement about a failing corporate care system had stemmed from a number of outcome studies, which had shown that large numbers of looked-after children and young people had ended up jobless, homeless and friendless. As evidence of just one of the major deficits in the children's services, a number of studies had highlighted the inability of children in care to benefit from the power of schools as a potential force for positive change in their lives.

In 1998, Jackson and Martin had written an influential article to illustrate the importance of the education dimension in the lives of looked-after young people. They had located and interviewed a group of high achievers who had grown up in care and confirmed the importance of educational success, as an important resilience-building factor that had helped children bounce back from adversity and to improve their life chances. Yet, as Jackson and Martin pointed out, many residential care staff were unaware of the potential power of education for the positive development of children in care:

> No facilities were provided for doing homework, there were seldom any books on the premises, few respondents could remember ever being read to by a member of staff. It was difficult to find a quiet space to read or work ...
> (Jackson and Martin, 1998, p. 577)

Bad practice may account for some of the failings highlighted by Jackson and Martin and the additional risk factor highlighted by Dent and Cameron but both studies had ignored the reality observed by Colin and his staff, that when the children arrived at the children's home, they were mostly unhappy, confused and angry, suffering from major attention and concentration difficulties, and exhibiting such violent and aggressive behaviour that it was a challenge to get them to settle to any activity, let alone more formal lessons in school.

While the academic view appeared to single out a failing care system as being responsible for the poor life trajectories of many looked-after children, the reality for care staff was that the children being placed in their care were troubled and troublesome *before* they came through the door.

> Taken as a whole, children in care have more difficulties when they enter care than most children. Most have experienced serious social disadvantage, abuse and neglect and other problems. As a result they have a far higher rate of emotional and behavioural difficulty, health problems, poorer educational performance and complex family relationships. (Forrester et al., 2008, p. 4)

In many children's homes, providing an academic learning environment, reading materials and opportunities for doing homework often may have seemed like secondary priorities when compared with the challenges for care staff of dealing with umpteen temper tantrums, systematic destruction, anger, and violence and extreme unhappiness.

It would seem that poorly trained carers not only had to deal with children traumatised by their previous neglect abuse and rejection but, perversely, these same carers had to deal with ill-informed public representatives and officials who sometimes used the simplistic correlations from published statistics and research to hold carers accountable for the natural but disruptive process of the children working through their traumatic pre-care experiences. Ignoring this was like arguing that the staff in fracture clinics were somehow responsible for the fact that the clinics are full of people with broken limbs!

However, the point where the research and the practice views began to converge was the significant mismatch between the National Vocational Qualification (NVQ) Level 3 training (which is the minimum requirement for all residential care staff) and the day-to-day practice skills which carers needed to work effectively with troubled and troublesome children. Clearly, the NVQ Level 3 curriculum, neither met the theoretical insights needed to work with these children nor the practical skills required to support them.

Concluding Comments

Our work on developing a model for professional childcare practice set out to offer a more grounded explanation for the continued poor outcomes of the children and to provide the knowledge base, training and empowerment for carers to address these. The link between our search for solutions and the impact of 'parenting' was serendipitous and followed concerns that had been raised by managers at the two children's homes regarding some staff practices, which were borderline inappropriate or which fell far short of the high, child-centred practices expected in the organisation. Indeed, a possible disciplinary action was being considered relating to one member of staff's angry response to a child who had poured a second glass of orange juice!

Following close scrutiny of the training received by our orange-juice hoarding staff member, we held a series of senior management team discussions throughout 2003. From these it was agreed that the chief guiding principle of good childcare in any setting should be *doing what good parents would do*. Clearly, a more objective and informed unpacking of exactly what 'good parenting' is, was needed, and this is the subject of the next chapter.

Time for Reflection

The true measure of a community's standing is how well that it attends to its children - their health and safety, their education, and sense of being loved, valued and included in the families and communities into which they are born. (UNICEF, 2007, p. 3)

What has happened to make us lose sight of this first priority in our society?

2
The Power of Parenting

Parenting: the bringing up of children by, or as by, a parent.

(Universal Dictionary)

It is possible to love a child passionately – but not in the way that he (she) needs to be loved.

(Alice Miller, US psychologist and author)

Having agreed with the management team at Colin's two children's homes that the most appropriate starting point was to tackle the question, 'what would good parents do?', we began to consider the concept of 'parenting' in more depth. Over the past few years in the world of public care, the word 'parenting' has been slowly replaced by the word 'care' (for example, as in foster care). Although there may be a few arguments of the 'valuing family ties' type for making this change, the essential 'parenting' dimension has got lost in the shift from a personal and individual focus to a more impersonal and quantifiable process: there is more than a subtle difference between being 'cared for' (a restricted set of tasks which a babysitter could be asked to carry out) and being 'parented' (a complicated process which involves not only nurturing, understanding and involvement, but also consistency, the setting of boundaries and appropriate expectations for behaviour).

Becoming a successful parent is a complex process for which society provides little or no formal training. It is influenced by a number of interacting factors including the natural skills and experience of the carer themselves, the characteristics of the children, the availability of an extended family, neighbourhood characteristics and the support (or constraints) of society. The responsibilities of being a parent are huge, especially since it has long been known that every aspect of a child's functioning – physical and mental health, intellectual and educational achievement and social behaviour – are all fundamentally affected by parenting practices.

Of course, parenting is often a source of deep and lasting satisfaction for parent and child alike, but there are also times when the tasks of being a parent are stressful, frustrating and emotionally overwhelming. Fortunately for everyone concerned, most parents and carers manage to overcome these challenges and go on to create happy and well-adjusted children and young people. However, for some parents some of these problems become insuperable and for a minority of children, home can become an unpredictable, frightening or dangerous place.

> Unseen in the background, fate was quietly slipping the lead into the boxing glove. (P.G. Wodehouse)

As many as two children are killed every week in the UK through parental neglect or abuse and 'the number of child deaths from abuse and neglect has not dropped in the UK in the last 30 years' (Creighton and Tissier, 2003). It also comes as a surprise to most people to find out that in England, the majority of the 60,000-plus children and young people in public care are there because they have been rejected, abused or neglected by their parents. Sadly, many of these children are likely to carry the emotional scars of such negative life experiences with them throughout their lives and, as a result, they achieve depressingly poor social, educational and economic outcomes.

> Sometimes, looking sad is met with friendly concern, and sometimes you are berated and punished for being ungrateful. But you just never know ... (Cameron child, Jessica, 1978)

Yet, despite its importance, parenting is one of those human activities which most people take for granted: most parents learn their skills from their own parents and through the experience of bringing up their own children. However, for professional care staff and foster carers who are often looking after particularly vulnerable children and young people, the skills and knowledge of parenting cannot be left to trial and error, but need to be unpacked, analysed, understood and implemented, often in difficult circumstances. Surprisingly, 'good parenting' merits only one mention in the Department of Health (2002) *Children's Homes: National Minimum Standards – Children's Home Regulations* (notably, in the context of respecting a child's wish for privacy) and is ignored in the otherwise thoughtful General Social Care Council's *Code of Practice for Social Care Workers* (2002).

In the case of residential care settings, much of the good practice would appear to result from the unspoken or 'tacit' knowledge possessed by care staff, rather than from their more formal, in-service training programmes. Even when the work of child carers is being done well, practitioners are unlikely to be aware of the specific elements and processes underpinning their good practice (see Anglin, 2004). Small wonder then, that the DfES publication on the proposed children's workforce strategy recommended more effective commissioning of services for children in public care which included paying greater attention to the skills and abilities of the workforce that would be employed in social care services (see DfES, 2005, p. 42, s. 3).

Our Starting Point: Parental Rejection

For the small group of children in our care the stark reality is that for a variety of reasons, their parents are not available to them. Although children in the children's home had their own ways of expressing this, each perceived their parents as having abandoned them. After more than a decade of research, Baumeister (2005) was able to conclude that the human brain's response to rejection was the same as its reaction to physical injury: rejection led to excluded people appearing to lose their motivation and willingness to make the efforts and sacrifices necessary to alter their behaviour according to the needs and prescriptions of others:

> the lack of emotion in our studies is not simply a result of people denying their feelings or being too embarrassed to admit them. Rather, it appears that their emotional system has genuinely shut down. They seem emotionally numb, not just to their recent rejection experience but also to the sufferings of others and to (relevant) events in the future. (Baumeister, 2005, p. 735)

When the source of rejection is a parent, then the effects on the child are particularly devastating and life changing. We now believe that addressing this trauma is the core task of residential and foster carers.

> [R]ejection is not simply one misfortune among many, nor just a bit of sad drama – it strikes at the heart of what the psyche is designed for. (Baumeister, 2005, p. 732)

Cross-cultural studies of the negative impact of parental rejection have been carried out over the last two decades by Ronald Rohner and his colleagues at the Centre for the Study of Parental Acceptance and Rejection at the University of Connecticut. Parental Acceptance–Rejection Theory (PARTheory) holds that *all* children need a specific form of positive response – *acceptance* – from parents and other primary caregivers. When this need is not satisfactorily met, children worldwide and regardless of variations in culture, gender, age, ethnicity or other such defining factors, tend to report themselves to be hostile and aggressive, dependent or defensively independent, impaired in their self-esteem and self-adequacy, emotionally unresponsive, mostly unstable, and holding a negative world view (Rohner et al., 2004).

A synopsis of PARTheory can be found in Table 2.1 and specific details of this explanatory model are available in Rohner (1986) or (2004).

Parental acceptance and rejection can be viewed as a high-to-low warmth dimension of parenting. This continuum is one on which all humans can be placed, because everyone in childhood has experienced love or (sadly) rejection at the hands of their major caregivers. One end of this continuum is marked by

Table 2.1 A Summary of Parental acceptance–rejection theory (PARTheory)

Main themes from PARTheory:

- Children need parental acceptance, not rejection
- Rejection can be clearly *evident* or it can be *perceived* by the child (although in the latter case, it may be less obvious to others)
- If the child's need for acceptance is unmet, emotional problems result
- Such resulting emotional problems appear to be universal, across the human race
- Some of these emotional and behaviour problems appear to persist in the long term
- Other factors are involved in the adjustment of children, but parental acceptance–rejection has been shown to be a particularly powerful influence on the emotional development of children

Source: Rohner (1986; 2004).

parental acceptance, which involves the warmth, affection, care and comfort that children can experience from their parents and other caregivers. The negative end refers to the absence (or the significant withdrawal) of positive feelings in parental behaviour and by the presence of a variety of physically and psychologically hurtful behaviours and affects. Thus, the warmth dimension is concerned with the quality of the affection bond between parents and their children, and with the physical, verbal and non-verbal behaviour of parents, which accompany these feelings.

An important and illuminating aspect of PARTheory is that parental rejection does not only consist of a specific set of actions by parents, but also includes those perceptions and beliefs that are held by the child or young person. Children who *experience* or *perceive* significant rejection are just as likely to feel ever-increasing anger, resentment and other destructive emotions that may become intensely painful. As a result, rejected children tend to suppress these painful emotions in an effort to protect themselves from the hurt of further rejection, that is, they become less emotionally responsive. In doing so, they often have problems with being able or willing to express affection and warmth and in knowing how to give, or even being capable of accepting, these positive emotions from others.

The strength of the Parental Acceptance–Rejection Theory lies in its insightful macro-perspective of parenting, its cross-cultural applicability and the effect of acceptance–rejection on other primary interpersonal relationships, including influencing these in later adult relationships. Empirical evidence now supports many of the major claims of this theory, especially the prediction that perceived parental rejection is likely to be universally associated with a specific form of psychological maladjustment, involving emotional, social, personal and other problems (Rohner, 1986; Rohner et al., 2004).

> [C]hildren and adults appear universally to organise their perceptions of parental acceptance–rejection around the same four classes of behaviour …

Table 2.2 Some examples of parental acceptance and rejection

Parental acceptance behaviour	Parental rejection behaviour
• Celebrating a child's achievements	• Ridiculing a child's achievements
• Showing affection	• Showing dislike
• Pointing up a child's progress and developmental milestones	• Comparing a child's progress unfavourably with a sibling or peer
• Spending special time with a child	• Too busy to spend time with a child
• Sharing a mutually enjoyable activity	• Imposing an activity on the child

> warmth-affection (or its opposite, coldness-lack of affection); hostility-aggression; indifference-neglect, and undifferentiated rejection ... Culture and ethnicity shape the specific words and behaviour (associated with these four categories). (Rohner, 2004, p. 830)

Returning to our previously mentioned professional disagreement about the major contributor to poor life outcomes for children and young people in public care, both authors are now convinced that parental rejection is the most likely culprit. Parental Acceptance–Rejection Theory challenges the uncritically accepted, conventional wisdom that the poor educational attainments, restricted social outcomes and diminished life chances of looked-after children, result mainly from the impact of the care and education systems, as some researchers have argued (cf. Jackson and Martin, 1998; Jackson and McParlin, 2006).

Unfortunately for parents and carers, the literature does not offer specific advice for promoting parental acceptance behaviour and for avoiding overt, passive or unintentional parental rejection. Rohner (2004) and Rohner et al. (2004) do, however, highlight the need for support professionals to enable parents and other caregivers to recognise and employ culturally appropriate ways of communicating warmth and affection and to avoid behaviours that indicate parental coldness and a lack of affection (for example, receiving a slice of Dad's apple or having hair carefully brushed by their mother versus receiving frequent put-down comments or being generally ignored by either parent). See Table 2.2 for further examples.

Our hypothesis is that children in care belong to a much larger overall group of dysfunctional children, with the common factor being the trauma of parental rejection, often accompanied by neglect and abuse. Yet, in all the UK literature on children in care, there is scarcely a passing reference to rejection in general or to parental rejection in particular.

Attunement and Secure Attachment

While the explanation of social and parental rejection has offered an explanation of emotional adjustment, it is *insecure attachment* that links the experience of

Table 2.3 Early attachment experiences and their effects on later development (cf. Svanberg, 1998)

'Secure' attachment
Trust in adults (cognitive and affective experiences integrated). High confidence, self-worth/social competence and interpersonal skills/higher school attainment at age 7 and better school adjustment

'Avoidant/Defensive' attachment
Trust component missing. Less socially competent/more internalising (e.g. withdrawal, non-participation) behaviour, more likely to victimise others at school

'Ambivalent' attachment
Deduction and anticipation dimension missing. More externalising behaviour (tantrums, whingeing)/more likely to be victims at school

'Disorganised' attachment
Both trust and confidence are lacking (vulnerability). Substantial learning and behavioural problems (especially aggression) occur in school

parental rejection to child behaviour, which can be wilful, hurtful, unresponsive, unfeeling and self-focused, and which often leads to personal unhappiness and unfulfilled potential.

The theory of attachment explains the crucial importance of parenting. A summary of the importance of the attachment process to the healthy development of the child was provided by John Bowlby, when he wrote:

> evidence is accumulating that human beings of all ages are happiest and able to deploy their talents to best advantage when they are confident that, standing behind them, there are one or more trusted persons who will come to their aid should difficulties arise. The person trusted, also known as an attachment figure, can be considered as providing his or her companion with a secure base from which to operate. (Bowlby, 1979, p. 103)

Table 2.3 gives an overview of different types of attachment, which can develop from such warmth, understanding and responsiveness, as well as from a lack of or a distortion of these experiences and also includes their likely outcomes for later development and well-being. (See also Grossman et al., 2005, for a useful account of the attachment process from infancy to adulthood.)

It is the quality of (usually) maternal care, which predicts the outcome for child security and adaptive emotional and social growth, and Fonagy (2003) has summarised the most important of these 'quality' attunement criteria as sensitivity to the child's needs, responsiveness to distress, moderate stimulation, non-intrusive behaviour, interactional synchrony and general warmth, understanding and responsiveness.

The process through which secure attachment develops is that of 'attunement'. Indeed, Parent–child attunement takes place when the adult not only understands

Table 2.4 Examples of carer–child emotional-attunement activities

- You take part in a fun activity together and laugh a lot
- You both talk enthusiastically about a planned future event
- You give the child in your care a spontaneous hug
- You ask the child to give you a quick hug
- When you tuck the child into bed, you go through all the enjoyable events shared during that day
- You spot something that the child is doing well and you let them know
- You spot that the child is a little unhappy and you sit down together and chat about this
- The child spontaneously shows affection to you and you respond warmly
- You enjoy a funny story together
- You inadvertently do or say something silly and you and the child sit down and have a good laugh about it (or you both retell the story to others)

The attunement process is most important in early childhood, but emotional attunement is also important for the healthy development of the older child

his or her own feelings, but can also 'read' the feelings and sensations which underlie the observable behaviour of the baby or young child and can respond in such a way that the child becomes aware that someone knows how to respond to their current needs (for example, to be comforted, stimulated or made physically comfortable). Howe (2005, p. 27) has described the significance of this process as follows: 'As carers help children to make sense of their own and other people's behaviour by recognising that lying behind behaviour are minds and mental states, a whole train of psychosocial benefits accrues, including emotional attunement, reflective function and emotional intelligence'.

Howe has reminded us that insecurely attached children often have parents who have problems in coping with their own needs of dependence and vulnerability, and therefore are poor at understanding either their own or others' thoughts, feelings, beliefs or desires:

> The family landscape is cold. It is a place of suffused tension. Warmth and spontaneous expressions of love and delight are rare. There is wariness. But lurking beneath the taut surface of everyday relationship dealings, there is also anger. Under increased stress, anger can suddenly erupt without warning into violence. (Howe, 2005, p. 91)

Experiencing an attuned relationship is a prerequisite to the development of both security and empathy in the young child. In other words, the roots of child or adult behaviour which is lacking in empathy towards others, or is socially exploitive or violent, are most likely to be found in early patterns which are established not only psychologically, but also at the physiological level of brain formation. It is the development of empathy, which is now being viewed as the antidote to both childhood and adult violence, an argument which is well evidenced in the Worldwide Alternatives to Violence report (2005). After all, how can someone be cruel or violent towards another person if she or he feels for the victim who would be affected?

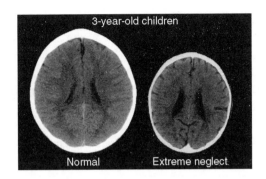

Figure 2.1 Brain scan images which illustrate the impact of neglect on the developing brain (www.childtrauma.org. Reproduced by kind permission of Dr Perry and the Child Trauma Academy).

The CT scan on the left is from a healthy 3-year-old child with an average head size (50th percentile). The image on the right is from a 3-year-old child following global neglect during early childhood. The brain is significantly smaller than average and has abnormal development of cortical, limbic and midbrain structures.

For over half a century, people working in the caring professions have been aware of the importance of secure attachment in the early years for the healthy development of every child. However, the adverse effect on a child who does not have the opportunity to develop such an attachment, although frequently documented, has often remained a subjective and speculative topic. Recent advances in neuropsychological research has confirmed that, in human development, the most rapidly changing of all the body systems is the brain: it is estimated that from birth until about age 7 our brains more than triple in size. Such research has also confirmed a clear link between essential childhood experiences like attunement or neglect and the healthy development of the human brain (see Gerhardt, 2004; Perry, 2000; Shore, 1997).

Recent advances in neuro-imaging and positron-emission tomography (PET) scanning, which allow the working brain to be visually observed, have confirmed the complexity of the developing human brain and its dependence on environmental factors. While physical injury and occasional deaths are clear evidence of abuse, the impact of rejection, psychological abuse and neglect has, until recently, remained open to debate. Bruce Perry, director of the US Child Trauma Academy, has produced dramatic visual evidence of the detrimental impact of neglect and abuse with his iconic presentation of two brain scans, one of the brain of a normal 3-year-old, the other of the damaged and underdeveloped brain of a 3-year-old child who has suffered extreme neglect and abuse (see Figure 2.1).

The new methods of measurement in neuropsychology and neurobiology which can quantify brain growth and activity have led researchers like Perry

(1997; 2000) to conclude that there is no specific biological determinant more powerful than a relationship in the early years and that early life experiences determine the core neurobiology of a child's development. For those particularly disadvantaged children who have also suffered neglect, violence and sexual or psychological abuse, the previously 'invisible' brain damage can be now be observed as 'grievous bodily harm'.

Going back to the commonly accepted position, that the care system is to blame for the poor outcomes of looked-after children, we can now include this physical evidence to support our hypothesis that the harm has almost invariably occurred prior to the children being placed in care.

While insecure attachment, especially in early childhood, can have major consequences for future development, it is important to recognise the astounding plasticity, flexibility and resilience of the developing child or young person (cf. Fonagy et al., 1994; Newman and Blackburn, 2002), even if the tasks of compensating for key experiences, which were either absent or abusive, generally become more difficult as a child grows up.

It is certainly the case that not all rejected, abused and neglected children become violent adults, and, as Perry (1997 p. 133) has pointed out, the majority of these victims are likely to 'carry their scars with them in other ways, usually in a profound emptiness, or emotionally destructive relationships, moving through life disconnected from others and robbed of their humanity'.

However, a more encouraging and optimistic perspective of possible life outcomes for children and young people, who have had negative and developmentally constraining life experiences, has been presented by Baumeister (2005) and it is this optimistic stance which we will pursue in this book:

> in many cases, rejection makes people suspicious, hostile and antisocial. But when a reassuringly safe prospect of forming a new bond does present itself, people who were recently excluded seem willing and even eager to take it.(p. 375)

The powerful influence of parents and carers in shaping children's emotional development is well documented by the positive outcomes for those who have received a high level of parental affection, thoughtfulness and understanding. The negative effects of neglectful or dysfunctional parenting are equally well established but, fortunately, there is also ample evidence of the effectiveness of parenting training programmes on the mental health of vulnerable children. (See Fonagy and Kurtz, 2002, for a 'what-works' review of this research, or Patterson et al., 2002, for a controlled study of the outcomes of the Webster-Stratton parenting programme delivered by health visitors to families of vulnerable children.)

Effective attachment-based interventions, which have had a positive impact on such problems, have either tried to help parents and carers to become more sensitive to child cues or attempted to change their beliefs about the nature of parenting. Not surprisingly, proactive approaches to child neglect and abuse are more likely to have positive outcomes, and cost-effectiveness, than reactive approaches, which serve only to pick up the emotional pieces afterwards.

Children who have not experienced an attuned relationship from at least one caring adult are likely to grow up failing to develop an appropriate level of self-worth and empathy towards others. It is no exaggeration to say that by ignoring the evidence of the traumatic effect of early neglect and abuse, we not only fail to safeguard the healthy emotional development of the individual child in need, but we also inadvertently assist in creating the next generation of, often violent, socially isolated and emotionally callous parents!

Parenting Style and Well-being

In the children's homes, one immediate effect of teaching these theories to care staff was the new insights which carers started to show in their reports on the children. Following discussions and training sessions, they were often able to offer thoughtful explanations for children's behaviour rather than getting upset and feeling helpless.

Our next task was to identify a common approach or style for staff to adopt which would be most helpful in working towards the outcomes identified in the national Every Child Matters agenda, namely: being healthy; staying safe; enjoying and achieving; making a positive contribution; and achieving economic well-being. For this common parenting approach, we looked for research which would demonstrate a clear link between 'parenting style' and positive outcomes for children in later life.

Nearly two decades of research by Baumrind and her colleagues have shown that there is a particular style of parenting – *authoritative parenting* – which reliably leads to positive development outcomes (cf. Baumrind, 1989; 1991; and Leung et al., 1998). 'Parenting style' refers to a combination of parental control and expectations for the child's learning and behaviour (*demanding-ness*) together with sensitivity to the child's needs (*responsiveness*). Baumrind (1991; 1993) identified four different parenting styles – *authoritative, authoritarian, over-indulgent and permissive/neglectful* – and these are illustrated in Figure 2.2.

Authoritative parents are able to maintain an effective balance between high expectations for their children and an appropriate level of control, responsiveness and care. Such parents establish and firmly reinforce rules and standards for their child's behaviour, constantly monitor these and use non-punitive methods of

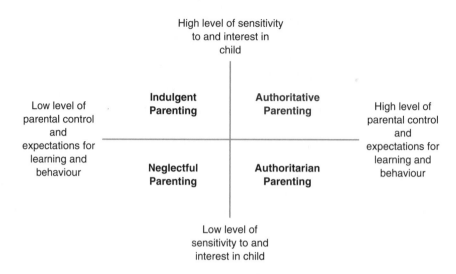

High level of sensitivity
to and interest in
child

Low level of
parental control
and
expectations for
learning and
behaviour

Indulgent Parenting	Authoritative Parenting
Neglectful Parenting	Authoritarian Parenting

High level of
parental control
and
expectations for
learning and
behaviour

Low level of
sensitivity to and
interest in child

Figure 2.2   Parenting styles in child care (cf. Baumrind, 1991; 1993)

discipline when rules are violated. While socially responsible and mature behaviour is expected and encouraged, authoritative parents are also warm and supportive. They encourage two-way communication, validate the child's individual point of view and recognise the rights of both parents and children (cf. Baumrind, 1991).

More recent work by Barber (1996) has added another facet to this parental style model – *psychological control*. This dimension stretches from the frequent employment of negative psychological control techniques (for example, using guilt, withdrawal of affection, shaming, emotional possessiveness, and so on) to positive methods of control like autonomy-building, seeking the child's opinion, understanding the child's needs and aspirations, using explanation and affirming the child's positive qualities. The study of 'emotionally harming' parenting is a relatively new research topic in contemporary psychology, and an excellent review of the issues in this area can be found in Iwaniec et al. (2007).

Therefore, the three major factors that define parenting style are as follows:

- *Responsiveness*: Baumrind (2005) views parental responsiveness as the extent to which parents pay attention to fostering individuality, self-regulation and self-assertion by being attuned, supportive and acquiescent to children's special needs and demands.
- *Demandingness*: these are the demands that parents make on their children to help them to become integrated into the family, together with the supervision and discipline required to ensure that these demands are carried out by the child.

Table 2.5 The three major dimensions of authoritative parenting and their likely outcomes for children

- The first of these – *parental responsiveness* – influences the degree to which a child can build trust in and develop empathy towards others
- The second dimension – *setting reasonable standards for behaviour and learning* – is concerned with the appropriateness and strictness of parental standards. Parents who practise a moderate level of control tend to set high performance standards and expect increasingly mature behaviour. Children who experience moderate control tend to be self-reliant, friendly and co-operative and to do well at school
- The third dimension – *psychological control* – highlights the importance of using positive forms of psychological control (e.g. reflection, learning from failure, encouragement, etc.) as opposed to sarcasm, belittling, unfavourable comparisons with others, guilt and put-downs. Children who experience positive psychological control are more likely to develop personal and social responsibility and to use rational argument, rather than intimidation, to influence the behaviour of others

Although it is recognised that parental style and child temperament interact, nevertheless, an authoritative style of parenting is most likely to lead to a high level of personal adjustment, self-management, social confidence and school attainment.

Authoritative parenting is only one type of parenting: sadly there is also indifferent, neglectful and authoritarian parenting.

- *Psychological control*: Barber (1996) defines this as control methods that influence the psychological and emotional development of the child. (Inappropriate psychological control is likely to involve bribes, humiliation, guilt, fear, exclusion or threats.)

Authoritative parenting is both responsive and purposefully 'restrictive', but in a way which is fair, clearly explained, consistent and balanced to take the needs of the parents and children into account. Authoritative parenting has been shown in a number of studies, both cross-sectional and longitudinal, to be associated with a robust self-concept for the child.

Concluding comments

In an ideal world, all parents would be closely attuned to their infants' needs, provide them with the essential early experiences which are required for healthy development and, as a result of such skilful parenting, violence, aggression and anti-social behaviour in children and young people would become rarer events than occur at present.

In order to ensure that carers can provide the type of parenting needed to ensure positive outcomes for children in care, professional carers need to recognise the needs of these children, understand the main factors which underpin successful parenting – the main issue – and direct their energies, skills and resources towards the causes rather than the symptoms of the problems faced by so many children and young people in public care. So, in order to understand what 'good' parents should be *doing*, in the next chapter we explain what we have identified to be the important pillars of successful parenting techniques.

Time for Reflection

Since research evidence points to parental acceptance as a key to the emotional and social well-being of children and young people and parental rejection has been shown to be implicated in their dysfunctional development, why has 'parenting' been left off the local and central government agendas for those children who are in public care?

3
The Pillars of Parenting

Corporate parenting emphasises the collective responsibility of Local Authorities to achieve good parenting. In broad terms, we expect a corporate parent to do at least what a good parent would do.
(Department for Education and Skills/Department of Health, 2000, s. 4.3)

Parenting is a complex activity that involves the integration of many specific behaviours that impact on immediate, medium- and long-term outcomes for the child (cf. Maccoby, 1999) so, for our teams of professional carers, identifying and developing a curriculum for 'good parenting' was the first big step in our journey towards an answer to the question, 'what would a good parent do?' There was no shortage of contributions from the managers of our two children's homes: indeed, we often ran out of time before ideas.

While this plethora of suggestions from managers may have confirmed our earlier assertion that everyone is an expert when it comes to parenting, it also raised other questions, especially, 'was it possible to take a professional and objective perspective of parenting, since we are so strongly influenced by our beliefs about parenting and our subjective experiences as children?' In short, how could we filter out the priority parenting tasks from the myriad of personal beliefs about what was meant by 'good parenting'?

Everyone involved in the everyday management of a children's home, is required to work within the *Children's Homes: National Minimum Standards – Children's Homes Regulations* (Department of Health, 2002). This key document details the requirements, procedures and policies that must be in place to ensure that children are safe, healthy and receiving appropriate support for their education.

While such standards represent a historically significant progression for UK children who are being cared for by the state, their antecedents can mainly be found in public inquiries into some of the more horrific child deaths, abuse and neglect cases, and therefore their recommendations are generally reactive, overcautious and focused on the (thankfully) tiny minority of children who have been severely ill-treated. In an attempt to prevent such tragedies, the 'minimum standards' have focused on procedures and record-keeping with the unintended consequences of diverting carers from direct contact with children to ensuring that the bureaucratic requirements are met. Like many legal approaches to problems, these standards of childcare, based on what had gone wrong in the past, can often get in the way of meeting the current and evolving emotional and social needs of children. Good childcare practice often appears to be drowning in the legal bathwater!

'Parenting' involves more than those activities that ensure a child's survival: its major objective has to be ensuring the development and well-being of children and young people. As previously mentioned, 'caring for' is not the same as 'caring about' and while the former can mean providing the physical necessities of life, like safety, food, clothes, warmth and somewhere to sleep, the process of 'caring about' demands a subtle form of parental involvement that includes availability, thoughtfulness, responsibility, guidance and emotional investment. 'Caring about' is a quality parenting process which is strangely absent from the ever-increasing dictates and advice issued by central and local government!

Identifying our Pillars of Parenting

According to the Children's Workforce Development Council (2007) parents and carers should be providing the following: basic care, safety and protection; emotional warmth and stability; and guidance, boundaries and stimulation. Such statements of intent may be laudable, but unfortunately they are too vague and unspecified to provide a framework for good practice for carers.

Similarly, Rohner (2004) and Rohner et al. (2005) have put forward some basic principles of parenting derived from Parent Acceptance–Rejection Theory (discussed in Chapter 2). Once again, these turn out to be broad guidelines, which would be difficult to incorporate into daily activities with children and young people since they include recommendations like enabling parents and caregivers to communicate love and affection to their children; helping parents/carers to identify and employ culturally appropriate ways of demonstrating acceptance; and ensuring that carers and parents can recognise the presence of perceived rejection in children who demonstrate a particular pattern of dysfunctional behaviour.

An examination of popular material on the subject of 'parenting' also served to highlight the need for selectivity as well as objectivity, since every author offered their own cherished answers to the question, 'what are the essential components of good parenting and how can these be provided?' In his book *Revolutionary Parenting* Barna (2007) has pointed out that there are 'more than 75,000 different parenting books currently at our disposal' (p. xi). Since popular writers like Barna, Steinberg (2004) and Kohn, (2005) appeared to be offering their own views of 'good and bad' parenting (Barna presents a Christian perspective), it was clear that we needed to develop criteria to cope with such an avalanche of ideas and to justify our selection of those essential, as opposed to optional (or, even, sometimes desirable) parenting skills.

Two major criteria for selecting our Pillars of Parenting was that it was relevant to understanding the needs of the children in our care, and that it was based on sound psychological theory and research. However, our selected pillars also had a few pragmatic criteria to meet, especially since the childcare staff insisted on the following requirements: relevance to everyday life, clear implications for high-quality childcare, promoting a proactive rather than reactive stance to children, providing a positive (as opposed to problem-focused approach) and being most likely to meet the psychological needs of children and young people in their care.

For the sake of convenience, the eight Pillars of Parenting which met the above criteria can be divided into three categories. These key parenting tasks are designed to enable and empower carers to ensure that their children achieve the following:

1 *Developing a sense of well-being: helping children and young people to feel good about themselves by*

- providing quality care and protection
- building warm relationships
- promoting an appropriate level of self-perception/self-worth
- ensuring a sense of belonging.

2 *Managing life events: enabling children and young people to respond to both difficulties and opportunities by*

- enhancing resilience
- teaching self-management skills.

3 *Acquiring social confidence and capital: helping children and young people to make and keep friends by*

- improving emotional competence
- developing personal and social responsibility.

In the following sections of this chapter, the importance of each of these Pillars of Parenting will be discussed, together with their implications for childcare practice. A summary of the eight Pillars of Parenting appears in Table 3.1 and an account of how the Pillars of Parenting link with the five Every Child Matters outcomes can be found in Table 3.2.

For each pillar, we have used the same descriptive framework. After a short introduction, we outline (1) the psychological theory that underpins the specific pillar, (2) a research and practice justification of why this specific pillar is so

Table 3.1 A summary of the psychological Pillars of Parenting

- *Providing primary care and protection.* This might include staff performances like offering reassurance in periods of distress either verbally or with a hug: attending to a child's appearance so that he or she feels 'good', and supporting attendance and homework to ensure continuing success at school
- *Encouraging secure attachment and building warm relationships.* For example, providing consistent and thoughtful staff consistency in behaviour management, engaging in play activities with the child and encouraging two-way communication
- *Promoting positive self-perception.* Examples here are helping the child or young person to develop a positive self-image, recognising and rewarding positive behaviour, protecting him or her from any forms of abuse or bullying, setting reasonable standards for learning and behaviour
- *Ensuring a sense of belonging.* The devastating effects of rejection, particularly parental rejection, highlight 'belonging' as a major psychological need. Developing this pillar can involve the staff in including extended family members, valuing cultural affiliations, building a child's personal identity and creating opportunities for shared fun and humour
- *Enhancing resilience.* Resilient individuals seem to have the ability to bounce back from adversity. Factors which are likely to enhance resilience in a child or young person include promoting friendships with school peers who are doing well, providing a key worker who acts as a mentor and offers consistent support and encouragement, and identifying and promoting a child's talents/assets
- *Teaching self-management skills.* Self-management is the insulation, which prevents inappropriate behaviour when enticing or compelling outside factors try to break through. Examples here include teaching self-managing behaviour, mentoring basic skills and encouraging on-task behaviour and self-reflection
- *Improving emotional competence.* Carers can support and encourage relationships with children and adults outside the family; teach the language of emotion and encourage the development of empathy (i.e. understanding the needs of others, as well as self)
- *Developing personal and social responsibility.* This lifelong process involves facilitating a sense of personal responsibility for others, accepting differences, treating people in a fair and valuing way and expecting the same treatment from others in return

© R.J. (Seán) Cameron and Colin Maginn (2008).

important, and (3) a 'theory into practice' section, which details the implications for everyday childcare practice.

Developing a Sense of Well-being: Helping Children and Young People to Feel Good about Themselves

Pillar 1: Providing Primary Care and Protection

In our affluent society it is easy to take for granted (and to underestimate) the importance of primary care, especially since our basic needs for food, shelter, warmth, sleep and health are usually catered for. However, as our managers working group pointed out, the absence or negligent disregard of primary care can be degrading, or at worst, life threatening, so it deserved its place as the first pillar.

Table 3.2 Links between the five Every Child Matters outcomes and the eight Pillars of Parenting

Every Child Matters (DfES, 2003) The five 'Change for Children' outcomes	Pillars of Parenting (Cameron and Maginn, 2008) The eight Pillars of Parenting outcomes for children and young people
• **Be healthy**	• Receiving **care and protection** *(Pillar 1)* • Experiencing **close relationships** *(Pillar 2)* • Building up **self-perception** *(Pillar 3)* • Developing **a sense of belonging** *(Pillar 4)* • Becoming **resilient** *(Pillar 5)* • Learning **self-management** *(Pillar 6)* • Improving **emotional competence** *(Pillar 7)* • Assuming **personal and social responsibility** *(Pillar 8)*
• **Stay safe**	• Receiving **care and protection** *(Pillar 1)* • Experiencing **close relationships** *(Pillar 2)* • Developing **a sense of belonging** *(Pillar 4)* • Assuming **personal and social responsibility** *(Pillar 8)*
• **Enjoy and achieve**	• Experiencing **close relationships** *(Pillar 2)* • Developing **a sense of belonging** *(Pillar 4)* • Becoming **resilient** *(Pillar 5)* • Learning **self-management** *(Pillar 6)* • Achieving **emotional competence** *(Pillar 7)* • Assuming **personal and social responsibility** *(Pillar 8)*
• **Make a positive contribution**	• Developing **a sense of belonging** *(Pillar 4)* • Achieving **emotional competence** *(Pillar 7)* • Asssuming **personal and social responsibility** *(Pillar 8)*
• **Achieve economic well-being**	• Building up **self-perception** *(Pillar 3)* • Becoming **resilient** *(Pillar 5)* • Learning **self-management** *(Pillar 6)* • Achieving **emotional competence** *(Pillar 7)* • Assuming **personal and social responsibility** *(Pillar 8)*

In addition to the need for protection, health, food and shelter in primary care, our managers included 'education' in this pillar, as success in school was viewed as a key to increasing life options, gaining employment and succeeding in our twenty-first century society.

The theory

In psychology, Maslow's (1971) well-known pyramid of human needs (see Figure 3.1) shows that people are driven to satisfy their needs based on ascending priorities, and the first priority is to meet our needs for primary care and protection. Maslow claimed that the ascending list of needs represented a hierarchy, where it was only when one group of needs were satisfied that people were motivated to move on to the next higher order of needs.

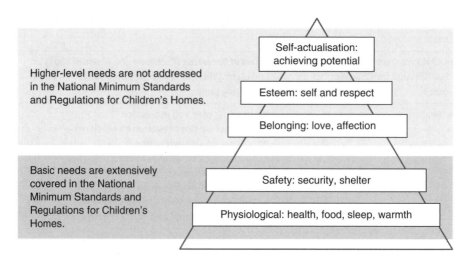

Figure 3.1 Outline of Maslow's hierarchy of needs

Why are 'care and protection' so important?

Of particular relevance to corporate childcare is the observation that most government objectives for looked-after children appear to aim at meeting the *lower* order of needs and to take little or no account of higher-order needs such as feeling of belonging, developing positive self-esteem, fulfilling our potential and so on. Indeed, a scrutiny of the *National Minimum Standards and Regulations for Children's Homes* (Department of Health, 2002) soon revealed that while the lower-level, physical needs for food, drink, shelter and safety were extensively specified, the important psychological needs (like self-esteem) were referred to only once, and belonging, love, self-actualisation, personal growth and fulfilment were not mentioned at all.

Theory into practice

Our discussions considered how providing for primary care needs for the children in our care could present an opportunity to subtly personalise each child's care in a way that communicated that he or she was valued. We can contrast a hastily prepared offering of oven chips with the provision of a well-presented, wholesome and child-friendly meal. Therefore, as well as maintaining standards and legalisation that specify bedroom dimensions, the vetting of staff and systems for making and recording complaints, care staff can also consider how their behaviour can help children to achieve higher-order need levels like belonging, affection, self-actualisation and well-being.

As a result of discussions with all the staff, a sample of specific activities, which were felt to underpin the 'care and protection' pillar, including the following:

- Tuning into a child's fears by listening carefully and responding in ways that recognise and reduce these fears.
- Taking calculated risks. Childhood involves exploration, taking risks and learning from occasional accidents and more frequent mistakes. Self-efficacy and self-confidence comes from the successful completion of challenging activities including climbing trees, playing conkers, kicking footballs, dancing, skateboarding and so on, and children in care need these opportunities to grow and learn.
- Attending to a child's appearance by ensuring that they are dressed cleanly, smartly, that their clothing is appropriate to ensure that they do not stand out from their peers and ensuring that they both look and feel good.
- Ensuring good health by providing age-appropriate health information and modelling healthy behaviour.
- Taking opportunities to ensure that the child succeeds in school by reading to them, or listening to individuals reading aloud, or showing an interest in what they are achieving in school, or helping with homework and developing effective communication with their teachers.
- Creating an 'achievement culture' in the home by celebrating personal successes and educational attainment.

Pillar 2: Encouraging Secure Attachment and Building Warm Relationships

All children who live in foster, adoptive or residential homes share the loss of, or separation from, their biological families. Additionally, many of these children will have had the experience of being rejected, neglected and abused by family members. Children in care often have parents who are poor at understanding the behaviour and needs of others in terms of their thoughts, feelings, beliefs, desires and hopes. Such parents are likely to carry unresolved issues from their own experiences of being parented and, sometimes, the behaviour of their own children can trigger these negative emotional reactions.

Fortunately, there is promising evidence that a number of interventions which are based on attachment theory, and which mostly have been carried out with parents of young children, can enhance the quality of the caregiver's interaction with the child (see Prior and Glaser, 2006).

The theory
The critical nature of parenting, especially in the first three years of a child's life, is now well established. In particular, it is the process of attunement between carer and child in the first 15 months of a child's life which results in secure emotional attachment and which fosters empathy in the child through its early experience of adult care.

Attachment theory was first outlined by Bowlby (1953) to explain the proximity-seeking, comfort-seeking and security-seeking behaviour of young children towards their mother in threat situations. All the evidence supports the view that children are most likely to grow and develop in environments where they experience several strong and close relationships. So, as Redler and Lucy (1995) have reminded us, attachment is not just any relationship, it is the key experience that connects the personal and social worlds of a child.

Svanberg (1998) summarises the likely healthy outcomes, which result from secure attachment, as follows:

> [S]ecure children learn to develop a balanced state of mind integrating both cognitive and affective memories into a coherent whole, to build trust that a care-giver will be available when needed and that protection will be forthcoming in situations of danger. (p. 546)

Bowlby's theory has stood the test of time remarkably well and current neurological studies are able to confirm both the positive impact of childcare (extensive development of neural pathways and brain growth) and the negative (lack of brain growth and development). A detailed and readable description of the impact the caring environment has on the developing child's brain and how this influences later behaviour can be found in Gerhardt (2004).

Within the context of the children in public care the following description by Howe captures the importance of attachment:

> The more secure children feel, the more time, energy and inclination they have to seek understanding and make sense. Whereas fear constricts, safety expands the range of exploration. This is why the social, emotional and cognitive development of abused and neglected children is so heavily compromised. They don't feel safe; they rarely relax. Fear for these children can be so endemic that exploration is weak, anxious and sporadic.(Howe, 2005, p. 3)

Why are 'close relationships' so important?

It was surprising, therefore, that several managers in our 'what would a good parent do?' discussion argued against forming close relationships with the children. Their (understandable) perspective was that since children's homes generally provide relativity short-term placements for children, it would be 'unkind' to get too close to a child, as she or he would have to endure a further separation when moving on and this might be perceived as yet another rejection. As we saw earlier in this chapter, this view is probably reinforced by the national guidelines and other local and central government advisory documents, which encourage carers to 'get on with the job' while maintaining a 'professional distance'.

The paradox here is that while some schools, children's homes and youth clubs have promoted a no-touching or minimal physical contact policy, current childcare theory and research would indicate that it is psychologically, emotionally and physically damaging for child to live in a world devoid of emotional closeness, lacking hugs, cuddles and other signs of affection.

However, encouraging carers to give and receive hugs is not without its complications, especially since during this period in our history, Social Services policy-makers have become preoccupied with child protection. As a result, many carers have become wary, lacking spontaneity and behaving unnaturally, in order to be seen to be maintaining a professional distance (see Piper and Smith, 2003). Ironically, such paranoia is unlikely to deter a determined abuser, yet it is clearly depriving children of positive contact, especially when a hug or a friendly hand on the shoulder can often convey affection, appreciation and valuing more effectively than words.

Theory into practice

For those children and young people who have only experienced unpredictable, neglectful, abusive or violent parenting, it may take a considerable amount of time and patience to enable them to develop trust in others, especially adults. The persistence required by care staff is likely to be only possible through their understanding the importance of close relationships and how these relationships shape a child's emotional development.

Particular tasks, which care staff recommended to support the 'building of warm relationships' pillar, included some of the following:

- Showing affection in as many appropriate ways as possible.
- Spending time playing with and sharing fun activities with the child. Apart from the sharing component, this time offers the opportunity to find out about the child and for the child to see a lighter side of staff members.
- Seeking opportunities to show the child that you care and that the child matters to you.
- Being consistent in your behaviour and your expectations for and of the child: this will serve to make your behaviour more predictable and understandable to the child.
- Tuning into the child's perspective of the world, thereby enabling the carer and the child to experience mutual empathy.

[T]aking vitamins helps fight off winter illnesses, such as colds and 'flu. Likewise, thinking about close relationships helps fight off life adversities, such as being confronted with failure or unfavourable evaluations. More succinctly, bringing to mind close relationships helps lessen the blow of stressful events. (Sedikides, 2005, p. 490).

Pillar 3: Promoting Positive Self-perception

Self-perception (also referred to as self-esteem, self-belief or self-worth) is a complex concept, but its influence on human behaviour is well documented. One study which has demonstrated the power of self-belief was been carried out by Avshalom et al. (2003), who found that children aged 3 who were rated as 'confident' were also rated 'extraverted' when they reached their mid-twenties and the opposite was true for very young children who were rated as 'inhibited'. As well as highlighting the persistence of self-worth throughout life, these authors also make a case for the setting up of early invention programmes to enhance self-esteem, especially for the inhibited group of children.

Many people who work in residential and foster care are only too aware of the low opinion which many children in care hold about themselves, even if they attempt to hide this low self-worth under a show of bravado or macho behaviour. Not surprisingly, therefore, there was undisputed staff agreement about the need to understand and build up every child's self-esteem and to include 'positive self-perception' as another key pillar of parenting.

As well as the rejection, neglect and abuse at home, every child in our care had gone through numerous 'placement breakdowns' before arriving at our children's homes. While stability of care should be a central aim of the whole care system, Jackson (2002) noted that the average number of placements increased during the period 1995–2000 and that 10 or more placements were not uncommon. She also goes on to remind us that lack of stability and continuity in care affects children's lives in a large number of crucial life dimensions, especially emotional development, education and attainment and mental health.

The theory

Positive self-perception or self-esteem, is included as an important human need in the Maslow hierarchy. He proposed two separate self-esteem needs (1) the need for respect and admiration of others and (2) the need for self-regard, in other words, perceiving oneself as competent and successful.

While Baumeister (2005) described the function of self-esteem as working to maintain positive self-views by processing feedback in a self-serving way, Cast and Burke (2002) claimed that the failure to achieve positive 'self-verification' results in distress. The later researchers viewed self-esteem as analogous to a 'reservoir of energy' that could act as a buffer against negative feedback, so an important care task would be to help the child build up the store of positive self-perception, so that discordant or hurtful feedback from others would be less distressing.

Research by Burnett (1999) provided support to the claim that an appreciation of self-worth has a major influence over what we do and say, and is affected, both positively and negatively, by how other people behave towards us. His extensive studies, using 'self-talk' as a measure (there is an established link between what people say to themselves and how they feel and behave), showed that 'significant others' such as parents, teachers and peers, had an impact on the child's self-perception. When the child perceived that the language of significant others was positive and valuing, he or she increased the level of positive self-talk and reduced negative self-talk. Conversely, the child who perceived that significant others talked negatively to them had a lower level of positive self-talk and a higher level of negative self-talk.

Interestingly, Burnett reported that boys were more affected by parental statements than girls, and the girls were more influenced by teachers' statements, than boys. However, the use of negative statements by other children was also a significant predictor of negative self-talk for both boys and girls.

Why is 'self-perception' so important?

What other people say about us and do to us can have a major influence on how we view ourselves. In particular, the impact that negative self-perception has on the life opportunities of children in public care makes this pillar very important. It is but a short journey for a child from perceiving that 'no one cares' to a position where the child stops caring as well. Low or negative self-perception spreads through every aspect of the child's life – why bother to brush teeth, get up for school, wear nice clothes, eat healthy food and so on? In a world where it does not matter, dropping out of school, indulging in risky, anti-social or criminal behaviour, getting involved in early sexual activity or prostitution, disregarding mental and physical health warnings, can seem like 'normality'.

Relating to the last point is the consideration that high esteem is not always accompanied by positive personal or social outcomes, psychologists and carers need to guard against the possibility that the self-perceived worth of some children and young people children may not be low ('I don't really like myself') but may correspond more closely to a belief that 'I can only feel good about myself when I am with X, or in place Y or doing activity Z'.

Jackson and McParlin (2006) noted that children leaving public care were four times more likely than others to require the help of mental health services; nine times more likely to have special needs requiring assessment, support or therapy; seven times more likely to misuse alcohol or drugs, and 50 times more likely to end up in prison. While all of these problems may not result directly from negative self-perception, a child's sense of self-worth is clearly one of the influencing factors.

Theory into practice

The sensitivity of the individual child varies considerably. For some, an unintentionally disparaging comment from a grandfather five years earlier, can leave an emotional scar, while an encouraging word from a teacher may have supported a child for years. Professional carers build up an intimate knowledge of the individual child in their care, so that these insights can be employed in subtle and thoughtful ways to ensure that the child is getting feedback which values, enhances and heals.

Staff-recommended tasks and activities, which underpin the 'self-perception' pillar, include the following:

- Recognising and valuing new skills as the child acquires these.
- Protecting the child from disapproval, teasing or bullying.
- Identifying the child's individual strengths then building on these.
- Making time to listen and understand what the child feels about him or herself.
- Encouraging the child to take responsibility and control over events and activities in their lives.
- Occasionally encouraging the child to try harder with the goal of enabling them to enjoy the experience of success after effort.
- Celebrating the child's developmental advances and achievements, recognising new skills.
- Setting high but achievable standards for learning.
- Being clear about and maintaining boundaries for behaviour.

When we reflect on the phrase 'being looked after' which labels the child as a passive recipient of services, we can begin to realise that language can be unintentionally pejorative and is unlikely to contribute to increased self-worth. The approach taken by the Pillars of Parenting is one which promotes belief in 'self-efficacy' in order to enable vulnerable children and young people to assume control over events and activities in their lives. Then, instead of a submissive acceptance, children will begin to believe that what they say and do matters. Such empowerment enables children and young people to recognise that they do not have to accept aspects of their lives which they would like to change.

Pillar 4: Ensuring a Sense of Belonging

Belonging is the third level of human needs in the Maslow hierarchy (after physiological needs and safety/security needs) and is viewed as a prerequisite for achieving a sense of self-worth and eventually self-actualisation. Families, friendship groups, schools and communities can all foster a sense of belonging: unfortunately, so can anti-social or criminal gangs which can often offer more attractive opportunities to belong than most foster and residential homes, schools, youth centres and work settings!

The theory

The need to belong begins early: we are born totally helpless/dependent. Survival depends on the mother providing for the baby's every need and responding to its cries of both comfort and discomfort. Researchers have now produced video evidence of babies, who are only a few hours old, mirroring the behaviour of their parents.

Baumeister's 'cultural animal' theory explains our need to belong as being shaped by nature specifically to create and sustain culture. The depth of this 'evolutionary' process is illustrated by our response to rejection, which he believes is similar to our response to pain or physical trauma:

> [A]s animals evolved to become more social, they used the same old physiological systems to monitor social events as for physical events. (Baumeister, 2005, p. 735)

Social identity theory (Tajfel and Turner, 1986) combines three key ideas: *categorisation* of people, including ourselves; *identification* (social identity and personal identity) and *social comparison* (evaluating ourselves with respect to other people). The process of social identity is not static but can change and evolve with experience as the review of social identity by Kroger (2004) has noted.

Putnan (2000) has advanced the idea of 'social capital' as an essential ingredient for communities across the world. Social capital refers to connections among an individual's social networks and the norms of reciprocity, tolerance and trustworthiness that arise from these. It is interaction that builds up a sense of belonging in family groups, friendship groups and communities (Putnam, 1995).

Why is 'a sense of belonging' so important?
The already mentioned research by Baumeister (2005) has highlighted the importance of belonging by pointing out that we humans are fundamentally social animals but that unlike other animals, which learn about their world through their five senses, we learn about the world from each other and enter into a social contract:

> People have all the selfish impulses of animals, yet if they can restrain these so as to follow rules, cooperate, and the like, they can gain the immense rewards of belonging to a cultural group. Human self-regulation is probably shaped by nature for the primary purpose of enabling people to restrain themselves so as to gain social acceptance. (Baumeister, 2005, p. 734)

While Baumeister's research on rejection has provided empirical evidence that the impact of rejection is both major and debilitating, a study by Hagerty and Williams (1999) found that the absence of a sense of belonging was also a predictor of depression. More optimistically, however, the need to belong could also act as a source of motivation and Gardner et al. (2002) found that their experimental subjects were able to selectively remove social rejection events from their memory, while consistently remembering acceptance experiences.

> [T]he need to be connected to others should lead most people to conclude that others rarely discriminate against them. Deciding that those who inhabit our social worlds treat us well, allows us to maintain a basic sense of belonging and connectedness. (Carvallo and Pelham, 2006, p. 96)

Our review of the negative effects of rejection had led us to conclude that the lack of a sense of belonging to family, friendship or cultural groups is likely to be at the core of the lack of motivation and subsequent maladaptive behaviours characteristic of so many children and young people in public care.

Theory into practice

A child arriving at a new foster home or children's home is likely to be experiencing the negative affects of rejection but, paradoxically, this could have the effect of making them more receptive to positive overtures from the new group. Making a child welcome, addressing their fears and anxieties, attending to their physical needs for food and helping them to feel safe, all make for 'good beginnings' in the process of bringing the child into the new social situation.

It is the carers' knowledge of the child and the child's own input that allows good childcare practice to be tailored to the specific needs of each child. The staff-recommended tasks and activities, which underpin the 'sense of belonging' pillar, include:

- Personalising bedroom accommodation by creating as many choices for the child as possible to give a clear message that the child's opinion is important and that he or she is a valued member of the group.
- Creating a home-from-home look in social and utility rooms. Children's homes, unlike ordinary family homes, are required to follow certain practices such as pinning up large red notices which state 'Fire Door – Keep Closed' or health and safety notices to remind staff to wash their hands, or registration and insurance certificates (in case one of the many official visitors need to check these). Part of our staff training has therefore involved the creative challenge of de-institutionalising our children's homes.
- Encouraging friendships both in and outside the home.
- Creating opportunities for fun and shared humour.
- Valuing the child's cultural affiliations/customs and so on.

So, the particular relevance of 'belonging' for children in public care is not only linked with the recognition of how all-pervading is the need to belong, but also shows how devastating social rejection can be in the lives of children and adults alike.

Managing Life Events: Ensuring that Children and Young People Can Deal with Both Difficulties and Opportunities

Pillar 5: Enhancing Resilience

Resilience was not a concept that readily came to the fore when selecting our Pillars of Parenting, but emerged from discussions on children who had been successfully incorporated into foster families, done well at school, found jobs and entered into long-term relationships. Carers had noted that the characteristics of these children and young people included a generally optimistic view of their futures, emotional flexibility and an ability to manage problems as these cropped up.

The concept of resilience has been neatly defined by Newman and Blackburn (2002) in their reader-friendly and practical paper for the Scottish Executive Education Department, when they write that resilience 'appears to be understood cross-culturally as the capacity to resist or bounce back from adversities' (p. 1).

An important property of resilience is that it enables us to shape our own future, rather than allow the effects of unpredictable events to determine the shape of our lives. It has been described by the Health Education Authority (1997) as 'the emotional and spiritual resilience which enables us to enjoy life and to survive pain, disappointment and sadness. It is a positive sense of well-being and an underlying belief in ourselves and others' (p. 7).

During the past decade there has been increasing interest in researching the factors associated with resilience, listing risk factors and adverse conditions, identifying protective factors and often then extrapolating these into strategies designed to enhance resilience, especially in vulnerable children and young people. Jackson and Martin (1998) in an influential study, which attempted to explain the all-too-frequent negative life outcomes of looked-after children, stressed the importance of resilience as a key factor that determined outcomes and concluded:

> Both negative and positive outcomes for looked-after children can best be understood in the light of the developing study of resilience. (p. 571)

The theory
Resilience is the concept that is used to describe the flexibility that allows certain children and young people who appear to be at risk, to bounce back from adversity, to cope with and manage major difficulties and disadvantages in life, and even to thrive in the face of what appear to be overwhelming odds. Resilient individuals, as Dent and Cameron (2003) explain:

[S]eem to be able to understand what has happened to them (insight), develop an understanding of what has happened to others (empathy) and experience a quality of life that is often denied to others (achievement). (p. 5)

One study which attempted to understand the concept of 'resilience' in more depth was carried out by Beasley et al. (2003) who conclude that the more resilient a person becomes, the more 'cognitive hardiness' he or she develops, and that children who manifest such 'cognitive hardiness' appear to share some of the following features:

- They hold a personal belief that they can control or influence many events in their lives.
- They view transition and change as a challenge rather than a setback.
- They recognise their own value, reflect on priorities and often think in terms of long-term rather than immediate goals.

More pragmatically, in their reader-friendly series of good practice books, *Assessing and Promoting Resilience in Vulnerable Children*, Daniel and Wassell (2002) listed the following six factors as being closely associated with resilience: a secure base; education; friendships; talents and interests; positive values; and social competencies.

Why is 'resilience' so important?
Jackson and Martin in their previously mentioned research, sought out and studied a group of *successful* people who had grown up in public care, and found evidence that educational attainment had been a crucial protective factor. Recent central and local government initiatives have picked up on this claim and made improved education opportunity a priority for looked-after children.

However, despite considerable financial investment, significant improvements in their educational outcomes for children in public care have proved elusive. An explanation for these disappointing results is indicated in the Dent and Cameron (2003) paper, where two psychological factors that appear to have been overlooked by policy-makers – secure attachment and authoritative parenting – are discussed. These authors argue that these psychological processes are important mediators between the early experiences of children in the home and the development of resilience or vulnerability, a conclusion that is supported by Daniel and Wassell (2005):

One of the key aspects that underpin prospective resilience is the presence of supportive parenting that promotes secure attachments. (p. 24)

It would appear then that personal qualities, supportive factors in the living environment and resilience-enhancing factors in school and community contexts are all factors which can enable children and young people to cope with major and negative life experiences like rejection, abuse and neglect (cf. Coleman and Hagell, 2007; Dent and Cameron, 2003) and that an over-concern with just one of these factors is less likely to achieve positive outcomes for vulnerable children and young people.

Theory into practice

In recent years a wealth of materials on 'resilience' has been generated to encourage good practice in teaching and childcare. The resource guide by Bostock (2004) for example, is designed to identify the key issues arising from resilience research findings and practice examples; produced by the Social Care Institute for Excellence it is downloadable from the publications section of their website (www.scie.org.uk). The Scottish Executive has also published useful documents, which attempt to convert the theory of resilience into informed practice with children and young people (Daniel and Wassell, 2002; 2005; Newman and Blackburn, 2002).

From our own children's home managers, the following represents part of a list of practical suggestions, which were put forward during our working group discussions:

- Ensuring stability and continuity in care.
- Promoting friendships with pupils who are doing well at school.
- Encouraging of high levels of intrinsic motivation and an internal locus of control.
- Locating one adult who can act as a mentor.
- Supporting regular attendance at school.
- Helping the child to read early and fluently.

In presenting their macro-model of resilience (which links the inner and outer worlds of the child, developmental theory and social work practice) Schofield and Beek (2005) have also been able to conclude that studies of resilience have now reached a stage where the focus of research has moved from factors to processes and that intervention has moved from identifying resilience to promoting and enhancing resilience.

Pillar 6: Teaching Self-management Skills

It has long been known that people employ a variety of strategies to enable them to take responsibility for, and exert personal control over, their own learning and behaviour. Reid (1996) has viewed self-regulation as the 'insulation' which protects cognitive and meta-cognitive approaches from 'shorting out' because of the intrusion of other factors like a drop in motivation, task difficulty, the effort involved or other distraction/temptation of alternative competing behaviours (for example, switching on the TV).

[P]erhaps the most valuable result of all education is the ability to make ourselves do the thing you have to do, when it ought to be done, whether you like it or not. It is the first lesson that ought to be learnt and however early a person's training begins, it is probably the last lesson a person learns thoroughly. (Attributed to Thomas Huxley, British naturalist, 1825–95).

The theory

Rather than seeing self-management as a fixed characteristic of children, most psychologists view it as a set of multidimensional processes that children have learned to use in context-specific situations. Zimmerman (1994), a long-term researcher in this field, has argued that self-regulatory processes are important in both the development of new skills and their application in real life. He described six processes that can be used for effective self-regulation, as follows: goal-setting and self-efficacy; task strategies; imagery and self-instruction; time management; self-monitoring, self-evaluation and self-rewarding; environmental (work context) structuring, and selective help/advice seeking.

Why is it important?

Good parenting includes teaching our children the skills to cope with both the challenges and the opportunities in life and preparing them for eventual independence. This 'self-management pillar' considers the psychological skills that are needed for the successful self-management of immediate tasks and to focus on future goals and aspirations.

Since it is one of the predictors of successful life outcomes, a significant area where self-management skills are required is that of academic achievement. Yet, we know that children in public care are significantly disadvantaged in this area, as it requires considerable effort and discipline on the part of a looked-after child to manage the distress of events which led to being placed in care, or to concentrate on preparing for an important examination when he or she knows that they may not be attending the same school next term, or in some cases, next week. The effects of such 'distractions' are not mitigated by intelligence or ability but instead serve to engender self-doubt, add to stress and further highlight the precariousness of being in public care.

One investigation by Lewis and Frydenberg (2002) noted the need to identify effective coping strategies, especially since the choice of strategies can have a direct bearing on health and well-being. Results from over a thousand students from various backgrounds in Melbourne confirmed their finding that children and young people should be helped to minimise the use of strategies such as worry, self-blame, keeping to self and tension reduction, while maximising the usage of strategies such as work hard, focus on solving the problem, seek relaxing diversions and seek physical recreation.

Theory to practice

Our care staff recommended the following as some of the care tasks needed to support the growth of self-management skills:

- Guiding and setting limits for behaviour.
- Employing positive psychological control strategies.
- Revising rules and expectations as the child or young person grows up.
- Mentoring basic skills, which can help child to achieve difficult tasks.
- Encouraging on-task behaviour/concentration.
- Teaching self-reflection.

Masten and Coatsworth (1998) have argued that we have much to learn from studies of resilience among children at risk since it is likely that the same factors will encourage development in both favourable and unfavourable environments and to enable children in general to cope with adversity.

Acquiring Social Confidence: Helping Children and Young People in Care to Make and Keep Friends

Pillar 7: Improving Emotional Competence

For the staff working in a children's home, 'good days' are special but infrequent, and emotionally draining days are all too common as carers have to face the daily evidence of children's pain through their temper tantrums, withdrawal, insensitivity and lack of trust in adults. Quite frequently our Pillars of Parenting working group would be interrupted by a call for the duty manager to help deal with incidents involving one particular child. It was not surprising that our discussions often focused on 'Danny' and his 'short-fuse' outbursts, violent behaviour, and apparent hypersensitivity to the word 'no' from an adult or a peer. Although Danny was 12 years old, one of the managers described his behaviour as 'still going through the terrible twos' and it was this insightful comment that helped us to recall that some children needed help in understanding and expressing their emotions.

The theory

There are several theoretical constructions of emotions, which include:

- The *relational model*, where Lazarus (1991) has appraised a variety of emotions in terms of their harmful or beneficial relationships between the individual and the environment.

- The *functionalist model,* in which Campos et al. (1994) have listed four factors that evoke an emotional response: the relationship of the event to our goals; the social response others give us; the pleasurable or painful affect resulting from the event; and our memories of similar earlier events.
- *The social-constructivist model,* which takes the position that our emotional experiences are the unique result of our social history, absorbed from our culture, our interactions with others and in particular, the reinforcement which we receive from significant others (see Armon-Jones, 1986; Harré and Gillett, 1994; Lewis and Michalson, 1983).

Banerjee (2005) has noted that it is difficult to pin down exactly what abilities, understanding and knowledge are responsible for positive social behaviour. His research has demonstrated significant links among all the following variables:

- Self-perception: judgement about one's own academic competence, physical appearance, social acceptance and global self-worth.
- Theory of mind: understanding how beliefs, feelings and intentions are linked to each other and how these account for people's behaviour.
- Attributional style: how we explain positive and negative events in our lives.
- Coping styles: these are beliefs about the kinds of strategies that can be used to help us feel better, especially after a negative event.
- Self-presentation: those strategies which enable us to control the way we appear to others.
- Role understanding: understanding the basis for and distinction between moral roles (for example, 'don't hit or bite') and conventional roles (for example, 'vacuum the kitchen floor after dropping a glass').
- Social anxiety: distress in (and avoidance of) social situations, and a fear of negative evaluations by others.
- Depressive symptoms: feelings of sadness and hopelessness.

However, it was the ideas of Saarni (1999) which we found most applicable to understanding the specific needs of the children in our care. Saarni detailed eight skills of emotional competence and devoted a chapter to each of the following:

1. Awareness of one's emotional state, including the possibility that one is experiencing multiple emotions.
2. The ability to discern others' emotions.
3. The ability to use the vocabulary of emotions.
4. The capacity for empathic and sympathetic involvement in others' emotional experiences.
5. The ability to realise that inner emotional states need not correspond to outer expressions.
6. The ability to use self-regulatory strategies to cope with distressing emotions.

7   The skill of reciprocity for sharing genuine emotions.
8   The capacity for emotional self-efficacy, that is, the acceptance of one's emotional experience balanced with your beliefs about how we live.

This developmental perspective treats emotional competence as being embedded in a cultural context and most children are socialised into this context by their parents. Looking specifically at the impact that parents have on children's emotional competence, Katz and Gottman (1993) found an association between mutually hostile interaction between parents and anti-social behaviour from their children in school. Havighurst et al. (2004) presented empirical evidence that children's emotional competence can be developed and improved, following a six-session parenting programme. Interestingly, both the children and the parents showed encouraging improvements, the children exhibited less emotional negativity and had significant reductions in difficult behaviour. The parents were more encouraging of their children's emotional expressions, used emotion-focused approaches more frequently in interactions with their children and were less critical and dismissive of their children's emotional expressions.

Why is 'emotional competence' so important?

Emotional competence is the ability to manage feelings and behaviour in a variety of interpersonal encounters. It underpins the successful development of relationships both within and outside the family, and there is increasing evidence that it may also moderate susceptibility to, and propensity for, later mental health problems.

Children like Danny may succeed in achieving their short-term demands with emotional outbursts, but the costs are great, as his behaviour was seen by other children as 'childish' so his social circle became limited as other children chose to avoid him. Additionally, carers sometimes had to restrict his choice of activities because of the danger to himself and to other children. One could speculate that unless Danny learned the skills of emotional competence, he might end up leading a lonely, loveless life with limited supportive contacts.

The importance of managing our emotions and resulting behaviour is further illuminated by Baumeister (2005):

> Certainly there is ample evidence that people who fail to self-regulate end up being rejected and excluded by others. Their spouses and lovers dump them, their employers fire them, their peers shun them, and in serious cases society expels them by throwing them into prison. (p. 734)

Theory into practice

The important message from research on emotional competence is that it is not predetermined, it is amenable to change and, as Saarni's work has demonstrated, emotional competence can be viewed as a collection of skills which, given input and the right social context, can be taught or acquired like any other set of skills.

After considerable debate and self-reflection, our own managers, agreed on the following list of practical suggestions for improving social competence:

- Understanding your own emotions. A good starting point for carers is developing the skills, which enable us to be aware of and understand our own emotions. Knowing the difference between sadness and fear, for example, will inform how we react. Self-awareness facilitates problem-solving and effective adaptations. Achieving emotional competence allows us to explain emotions and model appropriate behaviour to children.
- Understanding the child's emotions. The child's unique history holds the key to understanding their emotional states. Case notes will only offer a glimpse of this; there is no shortcut to spending time with the child, listening to what they say and building their trust – creating this 'attunement' with the child will enable them to develop an understanding of their emotional states in different situations.
- Teaching the language of emotion. Teaching children to understand their own emotions by using words to question and explain what the child is feeling. The skill is not in interpreting the child's emotional states but in giving them the language tools to enable them to verbalise their own unique feelings.
- Teaching empathy, for example, how do you think that Chris feels now? Empathy is the ability to see another person's perspective – it is a defining ingredient in being able to sustain a close relationship. Empathy is the single greatest inhibitor of the propensity to violence:

  [E]mpathy is shaped by how children see others responding to distress. By imitating the adult response, children develop a repertoire of empathy – or its absence. (WAVE, 2005, p. 23)

- Maintaining your adult role during any conflicts with the child. This demonstrates your own emotional competence, models appropriate behaviour for the child and being able to predict your appropriate response, and helps the child to feel safe as boundaries are maintained.
- Explaining why you want the child to do something. Providing a two-sentence rationale for your behaviour or request allows the child to assess your motivation and emotional state, the positive result of which is an understanding that you are being reasonable and that your request is fair (and not an attack).
- Respecting others' personal space and belongings.
- Looking out for the needs of others (children and colleagues) and articulating what you are doing.
- Apologising when you get it wrong!

Empathy appears to be at the core of emotional competence: the word itself comes from the German psychological term *Einfühlung*, which describes the ability to project one's self into another's thoughts. The main dimensions of empathy appear to be demonstrating that you can see the other person's point of view; accepting the feeling which accompanies this point of view; adopting the other person's perspective; and identifying directly (where appropriate) with the experience the other person is describing.

As children grow and are exposed to other children and the wider community, Saanri concludes: 'Given a healthy central nervous system and normal cognitive development, it seems fairly likely that favourable family, community, peer and sub-cultural contexts foster the individual's likelihood of acquiring emotional competence' (Saarni, 1999, p. 77).

Pillar 8: Developing Personal and Social Responsibility

Our working group frequently returned to the question, 'how do we teach children right from wrong?' Our final pillar of parenting sets out to address this issue of placing behaviour into a moral context. It is, of course, the role of 'good' parents to ensure that their children develop personal and social responsibility; however, this responsibility becomes emotionally charged when it is delegated (for whatever reason) to professional carers. There may be a clearly defined legal obligation to seek out parents' wishes with regard to religious practices, but the challenging task for our working group was to get a diverse group of staff to agree on an approach which addressed moral issues in an objective and rational manner.

How children develop social understanding has been a topic that has occupied psychologists for many decades. Essentially, the behaviours relating to personal and social responsibility ensure that a child or young person can meet his or her own needs in ways that do not violate the needs of others. Behind such behaviours, lie the principle of rights and responsibilities, a sense of fairness, recognition of the importance of reciprocity in our everyday lives and the wish to make a positive contribution to family, friendship group and community. Personal and social responsibility also includes attempts to solve problems in a peaceful way, understanding and valuing (and defending) differences in people and developing a sense of idealism.

Personal and social responsibility can involve acts like spotting another child's loneliness and not turning away from him or her, developing a capacity to reflect on the effect of one's own behaviour on both oneself and other people, and recognising that both self-beliefs and our judgements of other people can change. (A particularly useful reference source here is Carpendale and Lewis, 2006, who describe how children acquire social understanding.)

The theory

A well-known theory of moral development by Lawrence Kohlberg stems from the cognitive-developmental view that in human society, it is discussion which leads to a deeper understanding of moral dilemmas and which stimulates moral development (see Power et al., 1989). Kolhberg and his research group viewed moral development as stretching from an early (*pre-conventional*) phase (where children behave according to existing socially accepted norms because they are told to do so by an authoritative figure, like a carer) to a *conventional* phase (where moral behaviour is governed by what is seen as being in their best interests to gain the approval of others or, at a slightly later stage, because they feel it is their duty to do so). The final phase of the Kohlberg model (*the post-conventional phase*) regards people as doing things because of a genuine interest in the welfare of others, a phase which Kohlberg notes may often not be achieved by a minority of adults!

Kochanska (1991) who has studied the development of a moral conscience, has argued that it is affective processes, such as guilt or empathy, which underlie children's abilities to refrain from anti-social behaviours. A positive emotional relationship with parents is likely to lead to the child accepting many of their moral values.

Why is it important?

Essentially personal and social responsibility means being able to co-ordinate one's own perspective with that of others and behaving with thoughtfulness and/or fairness. Most people would not set out to be abandoned by their lovers, sacked by their employer, shunned by their peers or put into in prison, but sadly that is what the personal and social behaviour of too many children in public care may lead to. The background of many of the children who end up being placed in residential or foster care, is often a family life, where drug use is common, violence and sexual abuse are part of their everyday experience, and anti-police attitudes and a crime culture are the norm. Such children are likely to believe that it is the carers who live in a strange world and not themselves. Our enormous task is to re-educate and socialise these children into our a world where human dignity and kindness are valued and to convince them that the rewards of happiness, stability and leading a productive life within a community are preferable to a life inside the walls of a prison.

Carpendale and Lewis (2006) have argued that:

> interactions such as prudence or altruism can be conceived of as a form of morality on a small scale. Here, moral action has to be understood at the level of interpersonal, face-to-face interactions. This leads to the view that almost all interaction involves concern for others' feelings and wellbeing. Thus, in a sense the 'theory of mind' tradition may already have been studying morality without realizing it. (p. 225)

Theory into practice

Essentially the acid test of personal and social responsibility occurs when a child or young person faces a difficult choice and chooses the responsible, rather than the impetuous or irresponsible, option. Moral development therefore appears to be based on a combination of factors including knowledge, experience and beliefs.

The staff-recommended tasks and activities, which underpin the 'personal and social responsibility' pillar, include:

- Modelling considerate behaviour to others, as well as the child.
- Encouraging children to 'assume positive intent' for the behaviour of other adults and children. (For children who have experienced neglect or abuse, assuming 'evil intent' tends to be the normal practice.)
- Helping children to recognise 'stranger danger' from helpful adult behaviour: protecting children must always be a consideration as clearly not all adults have a positive intent.
- Model 'fair play' in everyday encounters with children and colleagues.
- Discuss relationships (work, leisure, sexual, and so on) as it is important to learn about the child's perspective and to gain insights into the child's beliefs in order to have informed strategies when responding to the child.
- Teaching children how to make informed 'decisions' puts them in control and allows them to evaluate the issues.
- Helping children to think about future aspirations and linking these to actions which the child can take today to help them work towards their aspirations.
- Enabling children to understand the key features of personal responsibility (for example, honesty and openness) and linking actions to consequences, which achieve desired outcomes or cause undesirable results.
- Introducing children to the concept of 'building up social capital', for example, doing something for a friend, helping someone in need or 'showing willing', without immediately expecting something in return.
- Developing global, as well as community and group, responsibility and altruism.

Concluding Comments

Although it has evolved into a useful working model, in one sense, the Pillars of Parenting and the associated staff support tasks will never be complete. Indeed, the addition of new pillars or the inclusion of new ideas and innovations is entirely in keeping with this approach, where the objective is to use the best available knowledge from psychology to address issues relating to each individual child's care and to ensure that the child achieves the best outcomes. In a nutshell, it is to provide the best possible answer to the key question with which we began this four-year quest: 'what would a good parent do?'

Time for Reflection

Whether you have direct or indirect contact with children, think about a child in your care, or a child you know well, then select one or two appropriate 'pillars'. Now, scan the 'staff actions' list and choose a few which are tailor-made for the parenting needs of child you have in mind.

Finally, can you come up with one or two specific actions that are not on the list. but which relate to the particular parenting needs of this individual child or young person?

4
Managing Challenging and Self-limiting Behaviour

Bringing up teenagers is like sweeping back ocean waves with a frizzled broom – the inundation of outside influences never stops. Whatever the lure – cars, easy money, cigarettes, drugs, booze, sex, crime – much that glitters along the shore has a thousand times the appeal of a parent's lecture.

(Mary Ellen Snodgrass, US author, born 1944)

Bringing a new life into the world may result in a number of joyous and memorable experiences, but it also places a number of important responsibilities on parents and carers, including the tasks of ensuring that children grow up to understand the limits and constraints of living in society, show respect towards other people and develop important benchmarks against which to measure their own behaviour. As far as parenting is concerned, these social rules and personal guidelines have to be introduced early, constantly reiterated and modelled by parents and carers as frequently as possible. Fortunately, for most children in most families, the process of enabling children and young people to acquire effective interpersonal skills, an understanding of the needs of others and a sound level of self-control, lead to satisfactory outcomes despite a few humps and bumps along the way.

However, for a small number, the joys of parenthood are short-lived as the demands of bringing up a young child become greater and the skills of the parent(s) do not (or are unable to) grow and adapt to meet these new child-rearing challenges. As a consequence, a minority of children in our society, do not get a chance to acquire these socially adaptive skills but learn socially dysfunctional behaviours instead, as a survey of 5,000 10- to 25-year-olds, for the Home Office by Wilson et al. (2006) has illustrated. In this study, they reported that 7 per cent of young people in their sample were guilty of anti-social behaviour during the previous year, the most common forms being assault and theft. It was also estimated that this small group of frequent offenders was responsible for around 83 per cent of all the offences reported in the survey!

Even within the population of very young children in the UK, there are those whose behaviour problems pose major management difficulties for parents and carers. Evidence collected by Thompson et al. (1996) indicates challenging behaviour levels of 15 per cent (mild), 6 per cent (moderate) and about 1 per cent (severe).

Children and young people in public care, including those living in children's homes, constitute a particularly vulnerable group, within which conduct, depressive and anxiety disorders are particularly common as a number of surveys, such as the one carried out by Nicholas et al. (2003) has shown. Similarly, in their study of children in care in Glasgow, Minnis and Del Priore (2001) found that about half the total group of children had emotional and behavioural difficulties that were serious enough to merit 'attention from professionals' (p. 29).

Carers in the children's homes in which the 'Authentic Warmth' model was pioneered were frequently faced by children whose behaviour ranged from vindictive to violent. In the case of children and young people in care, one result of such persistent challenging behaviour was that it slowly wore down the goodwill and understanding of staff, who would find it increasingly difficult to maintain a dispassionate perspective of what was going on and would often become less willing to be flexible and creative in their management of the situation.

While the four-region survey of morale carried out by Mainey and Crimmens (2006) found that levels of job satisfaction among residential care staff was generally good, despite the challenges of the job, one significant factor which impacted strongly on staff morale was the behaviour of children and young people in their care. Across all four regions, the issues of verbal abuse and violence were major concerns as were keeping order, managing anti-social behaviour and the safeguarding of other children and members of staff.

Contributing Factors

Hoghughi and Long (2004) have produced a revealing sequence of events that often lead to serious problem behaviour among children and young people and a version is reproduced in Figure 4.1. Although it can be seen that personal, school and community factors are likely to be important influences, it is family and home influences, which have been shown to be most closely and directly associated with the emergence of social, emotional and behavioural difficulties. For those children and young people in public care, these influences often include combinations of parental neglect, poor maternal and domestic care under the age of 5, family conflict, divorce and the absence of good relationships with either parent (Audit Commission, 1996). In families, some of the more subtle and less easy to identify factors which link early care and upbringing experiences with later challenging behaviour have now been uncovered: in particular, the absence of family support (Yoshikawa, 1994), dysfunctional family dynamics and beliefs (Gardner, 1992) and (as we saw in Chapter 2), parental rejection (Rohner, op.cit.) have all been strongly implicated in the emergence of children's behaviour problems.

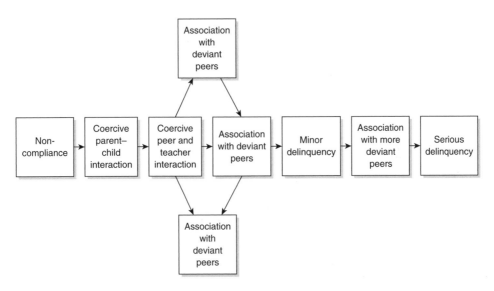

Figure 4.1 The trajectory for the development of deviant behaviours (adapted from Hoghughi and Long, 2004)

Research has also confirmed the frequently recognised connection between anti-social behaviour and external factors like economic hardship and low levels of parental educational attainment. However, even with such negative, extra-familial factors, it is their effect on the parents and carers (for example, a parent's irritable responses to discipline situations) that appears to be the mediating variable. In everyday language, a lack of money is only part of the problem. The literature review carried out by McLoyd (1990) presented evidence that depression, anxiety and irritability – all states that are heightened by economic hardship – increased the tendency of parents to be punitive, erratic, unilateral and generally non-supportive of their children. It is a telling point, too, that the majority of parents who are economically poor do *not* abuse, reject or neglect their children!

A small number of psychologists (for example, Pinker, 2002) have argued that aggressive and violent behaviour is an instinctive human response to obstacles to their immediate goal and that the basic instinct is to pursue our own desires, without considering the problems that these can cause for others. However, there is general agreement that most challenging behaviour results from emotionally damaging early experiences, inconsistent or neglectful parenting, and lack of opportunities to learn alternative and sophisticated interpersonal skills.

Children who have suffered inconsistent parenting often act on impulse, seek out thrill-enhanced experiences, pursue short-term interests, become self-centred and find difficulty in managing their own impulses. In other words, they are lacking in the very skills that could equip them to function effectively with others at school, work and other social environments.

A important piece in the challenging behaviour jigsaw is the converging evidence that aggressive and anti-social behaviour observed at an early age can continue into middle childhood and adolescence (see publications by Baumrind, 1991; Caspi et al., 1996; Gardner, 1992). If left unchecked, it is likely to develop into a stable tendency towards violent behaviour that will become increasingly resistant to intervention. (Mental Health Foundation, 1999).

Central Government Initiatives

Legally, a child or young person is considered to have (social) emotional and behavioural difficulties (SEBD) if they are 'withdrawn or isolated, disruptive and disturbing, hyperactive and lack concentration; those with immature social skills; and those presenting other challenging behaviours arising from other complex special needs' (DfES, 2001, p. 87).

Realising the increasing size of this social problem, and recognising the central role that the family plays in the development, maintenance and treatment of anti-social behaviour, a number of central government initiatives have re-examined the level of state support for parents (HM Treasury/DfES, 2005) and the need for local authorities to provide positive activities for young people (DfES, 2006). In the case of the support document, three underpinning principles are outlined: *rights and responsibility* – supporting parents to meet their responsibilities to their children; *progressive universalism* – support for all, with more support for those who need it most; and *prevention* – working to prevent poor outcomes for children, young people and their parents from developing in the first place (HM Treasury/DfES, 2005, p. 1).

The rights and responsibilities of parents and those who act *in loco parentis*, have been set out in a parent-friendly document produced by the Scottish Executive Justice Department (2003), which tackles a number of important questions including what can my children expect of me, what are my rights as a parent and what should I do when what my child wants is not what I want?

One of the most ambitious of the central government initiatives is *The Children's Plan* (DCSF, 2008), a summary of which appears in Table 4.1 and a section of which involves intensive help for some families and a parents' charter which specifies the minimum level of support which parents can expect from their local authority.

Effective Parenting

Teaching the basics of emotional control, interpersonal skills and social responsibility is a huge task for parents or parent substitutes, but a failure to teach very young children basic skills such as empathy, negotiation and compromise, makes them more likely to end up as anti-social, unhappy and often lonely adults.

Table 4.1 A summary of aims and actions outlined in the Children's Plan

---

- *Securing the well-being and health of children and young people* (e.g. intensive help for some families, new adventure playgrounds, a Child Health Strategy, a review of the Child and Adolescent Mental Health Service (CAMHS) and poverty reduction).
- *Safeguarding the young and vulnerable* (e.g. risks from inappropriate videos, exploitation from the commercial world, home safety, 20 mph zones, complaints procedure for children who experience bullying).
- *World-class achievement for all*, especially disadvantaged children (e.g. teaching based on stage, not age; partnership with parents; family learning encouragement; free early education and childcare for 2-year-olds in disadvantaged communities; every child a reader initiative; review of primary curriculum; extra support for special needs).
- *System reform (leadership and collaboration)* (e.g. all institutions achieving; world-class workforce; Master's level for teachers; challenge from local authorities for schools who are underperforming; general standards of behaviour; excluded pupils; world-class buildings; zero carbon rated schools).
- *Staying on: participation and achievement to 18 and beyond* (e.g. new forms of learning like apprenticeships; raising of the school leaving age to 17 years; new diplomas, e.g. science, languages and humanities; new regulator of qualifications; 16–19 learning to local authorities; 're-engage programmes' for 16-year-olds).
- *Keeping children and young people on the path to success* (e.g. improved services; positive activities programme; acceptable behaviour contracts; youth alcohol programmes; sex and relationships; youth crime action plan including, restorative justice; crime prevention).

Source: DCSF (2008).

As we have already seen in Chapter 2, the major within-the-home factor related to appropriate social behaviour is an authoritative parenting style (cf. Baumrind, 1991). This particular style refers to a combination of *sensitivity* and *responsiveness* to the child or young person's needs (such as will result from using the Pillars of Parenting component described in the previous chapter), *demandingness/expectations* for the child's behaviour, and *positive psychological control* in parent–child interactions. The latter two components relate to supervision, discipline and willingness to manage behavioural problems as these arise, together with the teaching of alternative social responses. During the past 50 years, researchers have established a strong link between an authoritative parenting style and later positive outcomes for children (see, for example, published papers by Baumrind, 1967; 1991; Lamborn et al., 1991; Leung et al., 1998).

Authoritative parenting is not just a creative and appealing idea; it is the only established styles of parenting which reliably leads to positive outcomes in the development of children Fortunately, authoritative parenting can be easily defined in terms of what parents and carers need to do: establish and firmly reinforce appropriate rules and standards for their child's behaviour, consistently monitor the behaviour of their offspring, and use non-punitive methods of discipline when rules are violated. While they expect and reinforce socially responsible behaviour, authoritative parents are also warm and supportive to their children. In particular, authoritative parents encourage two-way communication, they recognise and validate the child's individual point of view and ensure that both the rights of parents and children are recognised (Baumrind, 1991).

The message from the above studies is a clear one – authoritative parenting should begin in the early years! However, in the world of corporate care, most of the children and young people being looked after will have experienced a wide variety of parenting styles, ranging from neglectful, indulgent and authoritarian, to any combination of these. Many of these children will have been brought up by parents who make rigid demands, often accompanied by harsh punishment (see Gershoff, 2002, for a review of the negative effects of corporal punishment), while other children will have lived with parents whose behaviour was erratic, unpredictable and bizarre. As a result of their parenting experiences, a dismal majority of children and young people in the care system exhibit behaviour problems, which involve being aggressive, withdrawn, violent, cruel or manipulative.

In the heat of an emotionally explosive encounter, carers need a rule-of-thumb strategy, which will prevent injury and defuse a fraught situation, and such a quick-fix approach has been offered by writers like Moyer (1976) or Geen (1990). Moyer listed eight types of aggression which carers can be taught to recognise: these are predatory, inter-male, fear-induced, territorial, maternal, irritable, sex-related and instrumental or learned aggression. Correctly identifying which kind of aggression is operating can generate an appropriate, rapid-response strategy. For example, fear-induced aggression probably has its origins in the fight or flight response, therefore leaving the young person a way out is a better choice of action than keeping him or her cornered. With inter-male aggression, a non-threatening response by the adult male (hands in pockets and a soft voice) is more likely to reduce the level of aggression than a show of macho behaviour.

Instrumental or learned aggression is the most resistant to change, and for this behaviour, more careful thought and planning is usually required. Parents, carers and teachers begin to worry about their children when their behaviour persists in being *irrational* (behaviour, moods or attitudes which do not make sense, lack of apparent cause or behaviour which cannot be explained easily), *unpredictable* (alternating moods, unfriendliness and lack of co-operation) and *uncontrollable* (adults unable to impose authority and children unable or unwilling to control their own behaviour).

A general description of behaviour which elicits such adult emotions might be 'any behaviour which appears disturbing, dangerous or inappropriate to other people' but more pragmatically, the major types of challenging behaviour can be listed as follows:

- aggressive and violent behaviour (for example, hitting, kicking, spitting, throwing objects and often using abusive language)
- physically disruptive behaviour (for example, smashing or damaging or defacing objects)
- socially disruptive behaviour (for example, screaming, running away, annoying other children or exhibiting temper tantrums)

- authority-challenging behaviour (for example, refusing to carry out requests, exhibiting defiant verbal and non-verbal behaviour or using pejorative and racist language)
- self-limiting behaviour (for example, switching off during important tasks, using work avoidance strategies and refusing to take part in group activities)
- socially disturbing behaviour (for example, self-harming, sexually inappropriate behaviour or ritualistic behaviours).

The emotional reactions of parents and carers to such behaviour have remained a major area of study in psychology for the past hundred years. There are many ways of approaching the management of behaviour, some of which promise easy answers, for example, 'Supernanny' (Frost, 2005) and 'Mama Rock' (Rock and Graham, 2008), while other programmes tend to be more complicated and usually require a high level of outside support and monitoring.

A particularly creative, approach to building up parental discipline was that of Sanders et al. (2002) who targeted families in a 12-episode Australian TV series called *Families*. In this carefully evaluated study, parents in the TV-viewing group reported significantly lower levels of disruptive child behaviour and higher levels of perceived parenting competence. Clearly, such initiatives are to be encouraged, however, they have obvious limitations, especially since some of the most 'needy' parents, including those who use harsh punitive strategies or who neglect and/or abuse their children, are unlikely to take part in such training programmes, without considerable persuasion, incentives and external support.

One approach which applied psychology consultants have employed to enable parents and carers to consider the most likely factors associated with their child's problem behaviour and to generate strategies, to reduce disruption and to promote positive behaviour was that recommended by Westmacott and Cameron (1981). Their 'Antecedents – Background – Consequences' approach or the *ABC model of behaviour* enables supporting professionals to work with residential or foster carers in carrying out a systematic examination (or 'functional analysis') of the three most important dimensions surrounding any behaviour (whether 'good' or 'bad').

These three dimensions, illustrated in Figure 4.2, can be described as follows:

1   *Antecedents* (those events which precede problem behaviour). Such information can lead to the identification of strategies for the proactive, preventative management of potentially disruptive behaviour.
2   *Background* events (the setting or context in which the behaviour occurs). Data resulting from an examination of this aspect can lead to the creation of an environment that minimises disruption and encourages positive and adaptive behaviour.

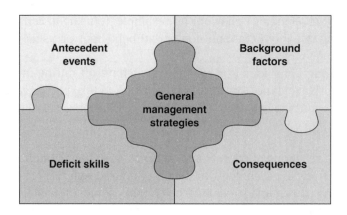

Figure 4.2   Using the ABC model to generate management strategies (after Westmacott and Cameron, 1981 and Cameron, 1998)

3   *Consequences* (those immediate and later events which follow a problem behaviour). Often this is the way in which the adult responds to the behaviour, so a careful consideration of consequences can generate more effective and positive adult management of a child's problem behaviour, after it has occurred.

Further details on the use of the functional analysis approach with children who have severe challenging behaviour can be found in O'Neill et al. (1990).

The advantage of the ABC model is that it is both simple and sophisticated, since it permits an examination of the complex relationship between behaviours (both positive and problematic) and the conditions, which influence these. Detailed information can be obtained by the consultant psychologist asking parents or carers to keep a record of the antecedents, the background and the consequences surrounding a particular problem behaviour and an example of a completed 'daily events record' for 7-year-old Matthew is reproduced in Table 4.2, together with Figure 4.3 which outlines improvements to current parental management (arising from an examination of the daily events record kept by Matthew's foster carers).

When attempting to interpret the information on Matthew's record chart, the psychology consultant, working in partnership with parents, is likely to find the following prompt questions useful in reaching a deeper understanding of the nature of the behaviour in designing improved management strategies.

- *When*, with *whom* and *where* does the behaviour happen?
- *When*, with *whom* and *where* does it **not** happen?
- *Which* consequences (especially adult attempts to manage the disruptive behaviour) appear to **increase** the frequency or intensity of the unwanted behaviour and which **strategies** reduce this behaviour?

Table 4.2 Collated summary of a daily record of Matthew's temper outbursts kept by his key worker and other staff

The Behaviour What did Matthew do?	Antecedents i.e. What do you think provoked it?	Background i.e. Where did it happen?	Consequences i.e. What did you do to stop it?	The Aftermath What happened as a result of your efforts?
Lay down on the floor and screamed.	Bill took one of his lorries.	In the living room after he came home from school.	Told him to go into the garden until he felt better.	He stopped screaming after five minutes.
Lay down on the floor and kicked.	I said 'Matthew clear away all your toys into the toy box.'	In the living room just before bedtime.	I ignored him and went to make myself a coffee.	He stopped screaming and kicking after ten minutes. It could have been longer.
Screamed and banged on the kitchen door.	Usual thing! Bill and Matthew wanted the same toy.	In the living room after school.	Sent them both to the garden to cool off.	Couldn't really say – they stopped very soon, say 3 to 4 minutes later.
Screamed and banged hard on the back door.	I asked him to come in from the garden out of the rain.	About half an hour later in the garden.	I sent him to bed. I'd had enough by then.	Stopped after about 5 minutes and then came downstairs okay.
Screamed and tried to hit Bill.	Bill broke his school pencil.	At the table in the living room.	Gave Bill a telling off and gave Matthew a hug.	The screaming went on for about 5 to 6 minutes.
Screamed and kicked me on the ankle. It hurt too!	I said he couldn't sit too near the tele.	After school while I made his tea.	I got cross and turned off the tele.	It lasted for almost a quarter of an hour. I thought it was forever.
Shouted and kicked on the piano.	Bill and Matthew were fighting about something.	In the living room just before bedtime.	Put both to bed and said I would read a story when the noise stopped.	I was amazed when I came up 5 minutes later Matthew was quiet and Bill was asleep.
Matthew went fishing with his dad all day. He was as good as gold. But what a week I've had!				

As a way of understanding the process more clearly, the reader may again like to scan Matthew's daily event record (Table 4.2) and the recommended strategies for managing his behaviour in Figure 4.3 then consider what would have been his or her *own recommendations* for improving the way that Matthew's foster carer(s)

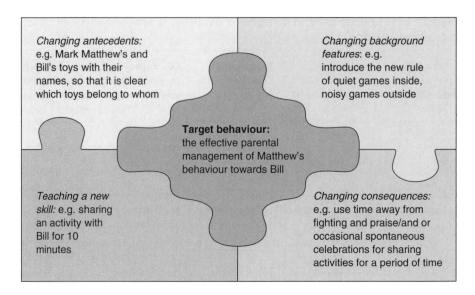

Figure 4.3 Using the ABC model to generate management strategies for Matthew (after Cameron, 1998)

might manage the behaviour of Matthew and (also that of his younger step-brother, Bill!).

To summarise, the ABC approach has the big advantage that it can be easily taught to parents and carers and can enable them to successfully manage many of the problems of individual children, including those children who have severe disabilities. As a result, many parents and carers have been able to use this approach to understand and manage their child's challenging behaviour and encourage the development of more desirable behaviour.

Behaviour as Communication: The ABC+C Model

The ABC approach is probably the easiest and most pragmatic starting point for managing challenging behaviour. However, some of the more worrying and disruptive behaviours of children and young people in care will have become well established, so it is more difficult to identify effective and low-response management strategies that work. When it comes to understanding and managing such persistent, anti-social or complex behaviour problems, it will be necessary for supporting professionals and carers to consider more carefully the motivational factor in such behaviour, and to focus additionally on its *communicative function*.

A key question, which the psychology consultant can pose is, *what particular need or desire is the child attempting to communicate/convey by his or her disruptive behaviour?* Identifying this need, which is so great that the child or young person has persisted with what is often self-defeating behaviour, is an important first step in developing a more effective management programme than is likely to emerge from restricting investigations to the behaviour only and those antecedent, background and consequent events which surround the unwanted behaviour. In short, after we have put in place those behaviour management strategies that work for the majority, for more persistent behaviour problems we may need to shift the focus to the child or young person's motives.

Although, the inclusion of a cognitive dimension of behaviour management was first advocated by Dreikurs and Soldz as early as 1964, it is only relatively recently that the power and utility of these ideas have been rediscovered by applied psychologists (see, for example, Cameron, 1998; Edwards and Watts, 2004). Like Dreikurs and his colleagues, these writers have argued that there were (at least) five frequently occurring 'reasons' why the challenging behaviour of children (and often, adults) took place, namely:

- *obtaining access to particular objects, situations or people* (for example, being with another person, carrying out preferred activity)
- *seeking attention* (initiating social contact)
- *exerting power and/or control* (for example returning to particular/preferred situations)
- *wishing to withdraw/escape* from a particular situation (for example increasing stimulation by escaping from boredom)
- *seeking revenge* (getting back at someone who has thwarted, refused, hurt or shown disrespect in some way).

As it is an extension of the ABC approach, this additional 'communication' dimension means that the improved model can be referred to as the *ABC+C model of behaviour* illustrated in Figure 4.4. It is this extra *C factor* that permits a detailed investigation of a child or young person's behaviour that not only illuminates some of the more subtle or difficult to spot antecedent, background and consequent events surrounding the problem behaviour, but can also highlight those appropriate skills for an individualised teaching programme, designed to reduce the problem behaviour or provide an alternative or competing response to reduce the duration and/or frequency of the unwanted behaviour.

In Figure 4.4 there is an illustrated example of how the ABC+C approach could be used to identify the key components of an individualised behaviour plan for Matthew, whose daily event record appeared earlier in Table 4.2 when the ABC model was used alone. While the ABC model can be seen as the foundation stone of behaviour management, Figure 4.5 illustrates the more informed and sophisticated management strategies which can be generated by the introduction of that additional *communication* factor (the ABC+C model) and the way that the *+C factor* can add an important additional dimension to the information available about the nature of the behaviour being exhibited by the child or young person.

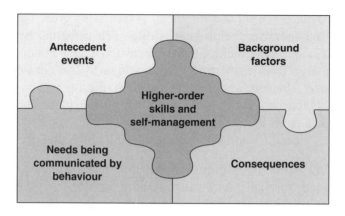

Figure 4.4   Using the ABC+C model (after Dreikurs et al., 1979 and Edwards and Watts, 2004)

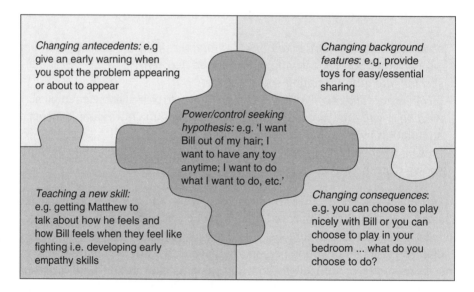

Figure 4.5   Using the ABC+C model to generate management strategies for Matthew (after Dreikurs and Soldz, 1964)

What emotional need do you think that Matthew was communicating by his behaviour?

To return to Matthew, our 8-year-old, the adults considered the list of possible messages, which Matthew's disruptive behaviour was attempting to convey, that is, the unspoken message being conveyed by his behaviour. After a short discussion, the foster carers and the pychologist finally plumped for a need for *power and control* as the most likely message.

Do you agree with this hypothesis, or have you got a better explanation for Matthew's problem behaviour?

In the light of this new information, what changes would you consider making to the A, B, C or + C factors so as to improve Matthew's problem behaviour?

What specific advice would you now offer Matthew's foster carers on the effective management of his behaviour at home?

And, just as important, which new skill would you recommend to Matthew's carers to help him to learn, so that he can cope better with Bill's interruptions in the future?

The example of Matthew (and Bill) was straightforward since there was a relatively clear reason for Matthew's disruptive behaviour and both children were still young and more likely to respond to adult authority. The problems of Jax, an adolescent with 'attitude' are more complex and difficult to manage. The account of the use of the ABC+C approach to understand and improve the carers' management of, and support for, Jax are summarised in Case study 4.1.

Case Study 4.1   Notes from a consultation session about Jax

These notes do not refer to one specific young person but are a composite made up from notes of several children.

(1) Jax's assets/positives, as noted by carers (and some other children)

- Thoughtful
- An engaging personality in a one-to-one encounter
- A reasonably high level of self-perception
- Can show unexpected 'wisdom' and insight into complex situations
- Generally Jax's behaviour is improving.

(2) Jax's problem behaviour

- Moody/sulking behaviour
- Likes to manipulative staff (and wind up other children)
- When she gets angry, she breaks objects or throws them at the wall

(3) Possible ABC controlling conditions for Jax's challenging behaviour

(a) *Antecedent events*

- Facial expression – tense, scowling, frowning expressions can signal an outburst. Also other signs of frustration like overactivity, unsettled behaviour and name-calling can be observed
- This behaviour often happens after requests to adults are not attended to immediately
- Jax is still missing her siblings and sometimes outbursts can occur after telephone contact with some of them

(b) *Background events*

- Usually in front of an audience
- Often moody and difficult in the mornings. Jax is not a good early morning riser!

(Continued)

(Continued)

    (c) *Consequences*

- Ignoring seems to be the most effective strategy for management
- Cajoling and humour can sometimes work

(4) Current management strategies used by care staff

    (a) *Antecedents*: trying to spot signs of annoyance/irritation/frustration and to divert Jax'sattention

    (b) *Background*: none identified/noted or discussed

    (c) *Consequences*: ignoring difficult behaviour and helping Jax to self-manage her own (fortunately decreasing) control problems. This strategy appears to be working well

(5) Communication (the +C factor)

What are the likely message(s) that Jax is communicating through her behaviour?

- 'I want to be able to control some of the adults in my life'
- 'I am missing my family'

(6) Possible additions to current management plan

    (a) *Antecedents*: when faced with Jax's disruptive behaviour, carers should adopt the belief/approach that this is the behaviour of an emotionally young 13-year-old who needs warmth and affection as well as management

    (b) *Background*: no suggested improvements: other child only occasionally involved and the early morning behaviour can be managed with minimal effort by adults

    (c) *Consequences*: continue to teach Jax self-management procedures, but add a 'reflection component' by prompting Jax to ask herself key anger management questions like

        – Is my current reaction a reasonable one?
        – Is this situation really important enough for me to get upset about?
        – What is the best way for me to handle this situation?

Use Jax's favourite/trusted member of staff (for example, Ali or Emma) to introduce these questions, so that Jax can use them to suss out a difficult situation and remain cool!

(7) Teaching a crucial new skill to Jax

The development of self-reflection: Ali or Emma can help Jax to recognise her own personal/interpersonal success by asking prompt questions like:

- What are some of the things I can do now that I couldn't do when I first came to live here
- Which adult has helped me the most (and how)?
- What other things do I need to bring into my life, which will make me happier?

The Management of Violent Behaviour

In general, settings like children's homes and schools have evolved organisational structures that support environments in which children and young people can feel valued, cared for and safe, and where disruptive behaviour can be managed with a minimum of fuss. Even among groups of children who are referred to as having social, emotional and behavioural difficulties, extreme acts of violence remain rare. Within this small group, a majority are likely to have faced a considerable degree of disadvantage and disturbance in their family lives, have special educational needs, lack skills in language, have literacy difficulties and cannot easily manage their own behaviour and emotions (cf. Ofsted, 2005).

For children and young people in general, the starting point for all emotional and social development programmes should be a positive approach to improving behaviour which creates opportunities for rewarding effort and application, and to build self-esteem (see Ofsted, 2005, s. 3.4). Such proactive management would include investigating why the child or young person behaves as he or she does, understanding the factors that influence this behaviour, and uncovering the early warning signs that indicate that disruptive behaviour is developing.

In the case of violent behaviour, Rae and Daly (2008) offer a specific programme to teach self-management and control of physically violent behaviour, however, active intervention would also involve trying to meet the young person's special needs, encouraging positive choices, developing his or her self-control, providing support for difficult situations and safely managing crises, if/when these occur.

However, for those children and young people whose behaviour is a risk to themselves, other children and to staff, two additional processes are involved in designing support programmes: *risk assessment* and *risk management.*

Risk assessment (see Ofsted, 2005, s. 4.3) involves a consideration of potential and actual risk. The Aggressive and Violent Behaviour Inventory (shown in Table 4.3) is designed to identify the type of challenging behaviours which are likely to occur and those contexts in which such behaviours are most likely to occur. No doubt, when she created this inventory, the author, Bailey, envisaged it being used as part of a structured interview with the child or young person, but it could also be completed by staff, who know the history of the child or young person, to provide verification of, and occasional discussion points arising from, the information already provided by the young person.

As well as a careful consideration of the nature of the challenging behaviour, the other components of the risk assessment process include the following:

- *assessing the context for risk* – trying to predict situations in which risks do/may occur
- *assessing the probability of risk* – trying to estimate how likely it is that the risk situation will occur and whether any injury or harm is likely (or unlikely) to occur

Table 4.3 Aggressive and Violent Behaviour Inventory

Questions for the child or young person	In home	In school	In the community
Has anyone ever thrown something at you?			
Have you thrown something at anyone else?			
Have you pushed, grabbed and shoved anyone?			
Have you slapped anyone?			
Have you tugged or pulled at anyone's hair?			
Have you bitten anyone?			
Have you punched anyone?			
Have you kicked anyone?			
Have you head-butted anyone?			
Have you kneed anyone?			
Have you ever put anybody in a headlock?			
Have you ever held onto anyone around their neck so that they might be starting to choke?			
Have you threatened anyone with a knife or any other object or weapon?			
Have you used a knife, weapon?			
Have you done anything else that might be considered violent?			

Source: Bailey (2002).

- *assessing the seriousness of the behaviour in question* – trying to gauge the kind of injury and harm that could result. For example, choking, bruises, bleeding, sprains, broken bones, stress and emotional burnout, panic attacks, nervous breakdowns and post-trauma stress disorder.

Risk reduction, on the other hand, involves an examination of risk management options and consideration of the benefits and drawbacks of each option for the child or young person, and for the others concerned. After weighing up the possible options available, some may be discarded as unsuitable; this will usually be because they have insufficient impact on the risk, or they contain too many drawbacks. A written record should be kept of risk reduction options examined and discounted, as well as those adopted for each child or young person.

The main risk reduction components (see Ofsted, 2005, s. 4.4) are as follows:

- *pro-active measures* to support the child effectively and to prevent difficulties emerging
- *early intervention* to help the child in difficult situations and to avert problems
- *planned reactive measures* to manage the child and others safely, when unavoidable difficulties arise.

Possible sanctions for serious or persistent misbehaviour could include being 'grounded', for a number of nights, completing a (meaningful) task which benefits the group, making restitution (for example, tidying up a room where objects have been smashed), or making amends to another child or group of children/staff.

The increasing use of 'restorative justice' has been a feature of the past few years. The term has been defined by the Youth Justice Board (2004) as exploring and repairing the harm caused by a criminal incident and consists of a structured process which can enable both perpetrators and victims to develop a deeper understanding of the background to the offence, its long-term and short-term effects and what is needed to repair the harm which has resulted. In children's residential care, Willmott (2007) has provided a promising account of how the restorative justice approach might be adapted to deal with the aftermath of conflicts and critical incidents that have involved violent acts and a short, but thoughtful summary of how restorative justice might be incorporated into the childcare system can be found in Hopkins (2008).

Physical Control and Restraint

When there is behaviour that is a risk to the child or young person, peers or staff, or is likely to result in serious damage to property, then the option of physical restraint may be considered (for further details, see DfES, 2003). This intervention is controversial and lies just outside the list of proscribed strategies which appear in the *Children's Homes: National Minimum Standards – Children's Home Regulations* (DoH, 2002, s. 17).

The choice of restraint as a behaviour management strategy requires careful planning, staff training, monitoring, record-keeping and frequent reviewing and the guidelines on 'Holding Safely' produced by the Scottish Institute for Residential Child Care (Davidson et al., 2005) outline the knowledge, skills, staff attitudes and supervision which underpin the use of restraint procedures, when these are absolutely necessary.

One particularly comprehensive and staff-friendly set of guidelines on staff management of behaviour in residential children's homes has been produced by Cambridgeshire County Council (2003). These guidelines, which have been written with regard to three important legal documents – Children's Home Regulations (2001), Human Rights Act (1998) and the United Nations Convention on the Rights of the Child (1991) – take a pragmatic view of control and restraint and argue that 'having to control children should not be seen as a failure, but as an integral part of good caring and therapy. It is part of good parenting' (Cambridgeshire County Council, 2003, s. 2.3).

Other Hard-edge Problems for Carers

Such problems have a number of characteristics including being discomforting for both staff and children, increasing staff concern and anxiety levels, arousing staff uncertainty about appropriate management and often requiring carer and multidisciplinary discussion and agreed action. Hard-edged problems exhibited by children and young people tend to be rare but they are also a source of considerable stress for carers, teachers and other children. In our discussions with residential care staff in a number of settings, the following list of what they perceived as 'hard-edged' problems in childcare emerged:

- physically violent (as opposed to aggressive) behaviour
- persistent absconding
- bullying, victimisation and intimidation
- frequent allegations of physical and sexual abuse by carers (these are viewed by residential carers as the 'most scary problems')
- compulsive lying
- severe attention-seeking behaviour
- spitting, 'gobbing' and pinching
- persistent racist/sexist comments
- 'disgusting' behaviour at the meal table
- the mismanagement of personal hygiene (including smearing).

Bringing out into the open and sharing these major sources of staff anxiety, discomfort and uncertainty can set the scene for an examination of the relevant psychological research and theory, which leads to the identification of good practice guidelines for discussion and continuing professional development for carers, managers and visiting support psychological consultants.

Concluding Comments

Although many books have been written on the subject, the reality is that there is no easy way of managing the challenging behaviour of children (or adults), but strategies that stand the best chance of succeeding are those where there is a theoretical base for the behaviour, some evidence-based research which supports the use of specific management strategies and the everyday activities of significant adults who know how to respond in a consistent way to the unwanted behaviour.

In this chapter, we have promoted a staged approach to the management of challenging behaviour by recommending low-response cost, low-energy expenditure and minimal intervention strategies as the most appropriate starting points for improving the behaviour of children and young people, before taking a tougher stance on the problem. That way we hope to enable residential and foster carers to avoid the ever-present temptation in fraught and frightening situations to 'take a pneumatic drill to crack an egg'!

Time for Reflection

Most central and local government documents relating to the disuptive and challenging behaviour of children and young people provide detailed descriptions of the constraints and limitations on residential and foster carers and the range of prohibited measures. Therefore, how *should* carers be tackling these problems?

5
Supporting Adaptive Emotional Development

In the depth of winter, I finally learned that within me there lay an invincible summer.
(Albert Camus, 1913–60, Algerian-born French author, philosopher and journalist)

The staff at the children's homes in which we developed the 'Authentic Warmth' model of childcare, often worked three eight-hour shifts, end to end: the late shift starting at 2 p.m. was often followed by a sleep-in duty, which usually meant spending the night at the children's home, followed by an early shift the next day before finishing at 3 p.m. Twenty-five hours away from family and home is an accepted feature of residential childcare and when things are going well, when children are showing progress, when the time spent together has included fun and affection as well as parenting and support, then that 25-hour shift was probably a personally, as well as a professionally, satisfying experience.

However, when carers have been subjected to verbal abuse, when some children have sabotaged all attempts to engage with them, when a particular child has discovered a new and painful strategy for inflicting insult or hurt, then sticking it out to the end of a shift and ending up in one piece (physically and mentally) must feel like one of life's little victories! Of course, experienced carers have learned how to use their off-shift time to reflect, recharge batteries, look at things from a wider perspective and come back refreshed for the next duty, but substitute parents are just like everyone else: they are hurt by rejection, get tired, hungry, angry and, just like the children they care for, like getting hugs and compliments.

However, parenting someone else's children also requires that, at the very least, carers do no harm, even when tired or angry (indeed, especially then) and have the responsibility to manage both the affection and the aggression they receive from children and young people, and to 'get it right' most of the time.

'Getting it right' when dealing with unpleasant, frightening and stressful behaviour is the essence of the 'Authentic Warmth' approach, and in Chapter 4, we provided strategies and techniques for managing challenging behaviour. In this chapter, we set such behaviour within the context of the children's emotional pain resulting from family rejection, neglect and abuse. Such knowledge enables carers to develop a deeper understanding of the frequently challenging behaviour of children in care, and helps carers to respond in an insightful and supportive manner to such behaviour. Such knowledge can help carers to understand that, for the most part, what the children do and say is not a personal attack, but observable evidence of the extreme level of emotional pain in their lives.

The Causes of Emotional Pain

Not all parents are able or willing to provide their children with the essential ingredients required for healthy development and, sadly, a minority of these parents reject, abuse and neglect their children. Children who have not received good parenting and/or have experienced negative events in their lives, are likely to have personal, social, emotional and learning difficulties, and too often go on to become part of a succeeding generation of aggressive, socially isolated and emotionally callous parents.

Knowing how to respond appropriately to this pain is an integral part of the substitute parent's job. In Chapter 2 we looked at the negative impact of social rejection and the even more devastating emotional effects when such rejection comes from parents. The use of the word 'pain' to describe the child's response to rejection, is no coincidence; indeed, recent advances in brain scanning have confirmed that social rejection and pain are processed in the same way and at the same location in the brain, and therefore 'share a common neuro-anatomical basis' (Eisenberger, 2006; Eisenberger et al., 2003). Readers will recall that Baumeister (2005) compared the reaction to social rejection to being 'a bit like getting hit on the head with a brick' and pointed to the similarities with our physiological responses to a painful injury – shock followed by numbness, then frustration, resentment and anger.

> Simply stated, children reflect the world in which they are raised. If that world is characterized by threat, chaos, unpredictability, fear and trauma, the brain will reflect that by altering the development of the neural systems involved in the stress and fear response. (Perry, 2000, p. 50)

These findings have implications for professional carers and suggest that not only will children and young people in care need authentically warm parenting, but they will also require the kind of emotional support that will aid the healing process. For many children and young people, a children's home or foster family can be viewed as a 'psychological accident and emergency service' which attempts to deal either with a seismic event that has resulted in an immediate care order or with the emotional effects of trauma suffered over a considerable period of time.

The importance of providing the right type of support at the right time has been highlighted by the difficult to dispute evidence which continues to show that observable outcomes for children who are looked after, continue to be poor compared to children in general (Department for Children, Schools and Families, 2008). However, in the wider context the link between the psychological and the physical dimensions of human beings has resulted in a re-evaluation of the many studies which link childhood trauma to adult hypochondria and psychosomatic illness, that is, patients who complain of varied physical symptoms that have no identifiable physical origin. See Waldinger et al. (2006) or Starcevic (2005) for a discussion of these issues.

In the case of children in public care, a more radical set of interventions than those detailed in the government White Paper *Care Matters: Time for Change* (DfES, 2007) is called for; at the least, more thoughtful consideration has to be given to the placement process to ensure that those caring for traumatised children have the skills (and the professional backup) to provide the support that they require). Similarly, on the basis that processes but not outcomes can be commissioned, the needs of children and young people in care should be assessed by professionals who know the research and theory relating to this client group, rather than undergoing an administrative assessment, based on what services and resources are available within the local budget.

Providing Sensitive Support

Everyone involved in the life-enhancing work of caring for these children and young people in the care system, needs to have the knowledge and skills to deal with the children's psychological trauma. Those homes where carers know how to provide the right response at the right time, stand out from homes that provide a glorified bed and breakfast service (with token emotional support and a high level of risk-averse, but politically correct, practice). The best homes are those where carers can use up-to-date psychological knowledge to help a child through a difficult and painful period of their lives using sensitivity, consistency, clear boundaries, perceived warmth and help which enables children to find their inner strengths and use their talents in the pursuit of fulfilment in life.

In this chapter, we explain how the adaptive emotional development component of the 'Authentic Warmth' model of professional childcare can help substitute parents understand and respond to children's pain while protecting themselves from the more stressful aspects of this work. We do this by looking at three areas with observations on how a consultant psychologist can provide professional support in each of these.

1   *Knowledge and insight.* We have adapted the three-stage model of the journey through traumatic stress from the book *Attachment, Trauma and Resilience* (Cairns, 2002) to help us understand and respond to the different stages of recovery from trauma.

2 *The recovery trajectory.* Recognising and understanding the different reaction trajectories that follow longer-term rejection, abuse and neglect, and the different types of support which may be required for each of these.
3 *Post-traumatic growth.* The 'Authentic Warmth' approach has been designed to move beyond the traditional goal of professional parenting – helping children and young people to cope – to the new position, post-traumatic *growth*, where we seek to build on the children's strengths, skills and positive qualities and help our children on their journey from pain to recovery and, finally, to rediscovery (cf. Joseph and Linley, 2008).

Knowledge and Insight

Even the most empathic and observant carer can only gain glimpses of the emotional pain and suffering which results from rejection, neglect and abuse. Just as each child is unique, so too are their experiences and responses. We can learn from the experience, reflection and research of others; for example, Cairns (2002) provides touching insights into the daily drama of looking after traumatised children. Further insights into children's pain can be obtained from first-hand accounts of abusive childhoods, from the many books in this genre. In *A child called 'IT'* Pelzer (1995) illustrates the lengths to which some disturbed parents are prepared to go to humiliate and abuse their children and also the depth of the emotional hurt which many children experience as a result of such treatment. Landon's (2007) book *Daddy's Little Earner* tells the harrowing story of how her father forced her into prostitution at an early age.

At Bristol Crown Court in April 2007, 62-year-old Eunice Spry (a foster carer) was sentenced to 14 years in prison for the systematic wounding, cruelty and assault of children in her care, and the story of this abuse is told separately by two of the children who had been in her care, *Child C: Surviving a Foster Mother's Reign of Terror* (Spry, 2008) and *Deliver Me from Evil* (Gilbert, 2008).

Such material may provide carers with insights into how important and significant even small acts of kindness can be to a child, and highlights the prevalence of child abuse and neglect and its devastating consequences, confirming the critical need for a skilled, caring and informed children's workforce.

To support individual children on their difficult journey from post-trauma unhappiness to being able to love and learn again, carers have to be able to conceptualise the emotional problems and pitfalls that children encounter along the way. The 'river of life' slide, an original and powerful idea from Dr Richard Wilson, a consultant paediatrician at Kingston Hospital in Surrey, has been used in a number of training sessions for carers and managers (Figure 5.1) and rarely failed to provoke surprise and optimism among participants. A frequent outcome of these

**The River of Life, The Waterfall of Trauma,
The Whirlpool of Grief and The Moreplacid Pools of Optimism**

Figure 5.1 The emotional journey from trauma to tranquillity. Reproduced by kind permission of Dr Richard Wilson, Kingston Hospital, Surrey, and drawn by David Thomas, Head of Art at Peter Symonds College, Winchester

discussions has been a reinterpretation of the behaviour of one or two particularly difficult to manage children from viewing what they do as ingrained and vindictive, with little hope for change, to an acknowledgement of their emotional pain, the possibility of adaptive emotional development (*things can change*) and a consideration of strategies which could be used to support children better in the future.

An early description of the series of emotional states which were likely to follow traumatic events emerged from the observations of young children made by Bowlby (1961) who noted four stages in the recovery process: shock/numbness, yearning/searching, disorganisation/despair and eventual reorganisation. Later, Kubler-Ross in her interviews with traumatised terminally-ill patients, listed five stages: denial, anger, bargaining, depression and acceptance (see Kubler-Ross and Kessler, 2007, for a summary of this).

Based on her first-hand experience with foster children, Cairns (2002), has moved beyond explanation to generate advice on the type of support and management that is likely to be required for working with traumatised children at different stages of their post-trauma adjustment. She has also recognised the emotional demands on carers, who provide the support needed by such children and makes a clear statement about the level of commitment required: 'If you are unable to offer this commitment, do not undertake this work' (p. 68).

In the Cairns model, the post-traumatic stress process has been simplified into three key stages or phases – *stabilisation*, *integration* and *adaptation* – each of which has three general support activities. An overview has been provided in Table 5.1, together with some good practice from a longer menu of support activities, which our carers and managers have listed for possible everyday use. Similar to the way in which the staff activities which supported the Pillars of Parenting were obtained, the support activities of the 'adaptive emotional development' component resulted from contributions drawn from the previous experience of carers

Table 5.1 The Cairns model of emotional adaptation, together with suggested actions by carers to support a child or young person at the different stages towards adaptive emotional development

Stabilisation *(Providing a safe and predictable physical and psychological environment)*	Integration *(Aiding a child or young person in the processing of the trauma, i.e. putting the past in its place)*	Adaptation *(Enabling the re-establishment of social connectedness, personal efficacy and the rediscovering of the joy of living)*
Suggested actions by carers:	Suggested actions by carers:	Suggested actions by carers:
• Establishing a clear and predictable pattern of daily events for the child	• Stressing the normality of feelings associated with previous traumatic events	• Helping the child to accept some of the life changes which have occurred
• Protecting the child from teasing, bullying and intimidation	• When naturally occurring opportunities arise, encouraging children to talk about events in their life and their feelings towards these	• Supporting the child's own efforts to adapt to the changed circumstances
• Creating a sense of belonging (e.g. personal room decorations, choice of clothes, etc.)	• Responding to such opportunities in a sensitive, valuing and age-appropriate manner	• Gently challenging dysfunctional or inappropriate attributions for negative events experienced by the child
• Behaving in an open, valuing and predictable way towards the child or young person	• Becoming a good role model by articulating your own feelings about events in your life or the life of others, as these naturally arise	• Reminding the child about those areas where he or she can control events in his or her life
• Reassuring the child that the staff are friendly and will listen to children	• Stressing the 'normality' of sadness, anger, guilt, regret and other painful feelings relating to traumatic events, which are being expressed by the child	• Helping the child to accept that there may be some things which people do, or some events in life that happen and which are never fully understood which we may need to accept and learn to 'live with'
• Beginning to form a relationship with the child	• Managing the child's strong emotions, e.g. grief,	• Offering hope … things can change, things can get better

(Continued)

Table 5.1   (Continued)

Stabilisation (Providing a safe and predictable physical and psychological environment)	Integration (Aiding a child or young person in the processing of the trauma, i.e. putting the past in its place)	Adaptation (Enabling the re-establishment of social connectedness, personal efficacy and the rediscovering of the joy of living)
	emotional pain, fear, bewilderment, by offering appropriate reassurance	… and that post-traumatic growth is possible
• Establishing a clear and predictable pattern of daily events to foster feelings of security	• Trying to understand the source of a child's disruptive behaviour before choosing/administering the consequences	
• Providing clear rules for behaviour towards staff and other children and applying these fairly to all	• Managing the child's sense of guilt, or responsibility for what has happened	
• Offering spontaneous affection or praise	• Praising the child for having the courage to talk about emotionally difficult issues	
• Building in 'quality encounters' with the child or young person	• Being prepared to repeat information several times as the child processes this	
• Offering choices to give the child control over events in his or her life		
• Watching out for signs of anxiety and distress (e.g. avoidance of peers and staff, spending long terms alone, disturbed sleep patterns)		

Source: Cairns (2002).

and managers, some contributions from the psychologist consultant and informal conversations with the children and young people themselves on the themes of 'what makes you unhappy and what is it that helps you to feel happier again?'

The advantage of the Cairns model is that it can provide a clear, but sophisticated, framework for understanding the progression from trauma-induced stress to recovery, which can be used for the practical training and consultation sessions with the direct carers. While all of the three stages need careful discussion and reflection, it is the 'integration' phase which presents the biggest challenges to carers and consultant alike. In psychological terms the task here is to help the child or young person to cognitively process the emotional impact of the traumatic events and to enable the child to find ways of adapting to these so that they can be assimilated into his or her cognitive schemata and the child can move on to respond to current and more positive events. In carer terms, the task is to allow the child to find an emotional explanation for what has happened, so that he or she can 'move on'.

The task for the psychologist consultant is to combine the (often impressive) carers' knowledge and insights relating to an individual child with the theory and research from the knowledge base in psychology. Done well, this can result in a support plan which is tailor-made for a particular child at a particular point in time, encourages the creative application of psychology, yet retains a practical and pragmatic component which ensures that the advice can be applied to everyday encounters with the child or young person concerned. On the prevention side, such a support plan can prevent the build-up of self-defeating behaviours and beliefs, including self-isolation, self-blame, avoidance (for example, 'escaping' into alcohol and drug abuse) or blaming others for the everyday problems which crop up.

Preparation of the support plan can also provide an opportunity for the psychologist to highlight the difference between a professional response and the well-intended, but usually unhelpful, everyday statements such as 'I know how you feel' (when no one else can really know) or 'It's OK now' (when it is clearly not OK). Indeed, care must be taken to ensure that the situation is not inadvertently made worse by a carer's ill-considered or thoughtless remark.

Central to the 'Authentic Warmth' model is the recognition of the individuality of each child or young person: every child is unique, as is their response to trauma. What the adaptive emotional development component of the 'Authentic Warmth' approach allows is a functional, but general, understanding of the adaptation process; it is the staff activity menu which provides the carefully considered and selected staff responses that are required to meet the specific needs of the individual.

Post-trauma Reaction Trajectories

It also has to be recognised that children and young people who have experienced major negative life events can react in diverse ways. Many are severely affected by the events in their lives, some less so, and other more resilient individuals may show no apparent disruption in their ability to function and seem to be able to move on to tackle new life challenges as these arise. While some experts may hold the view that such ease of adjustment is attributable to 'denial' or a 'delayed grief reaction' (cf. Middleton et al., 1996) a more optimistic perspective has been presented by Bonanno and Mancini (2008) who have argued that the human race

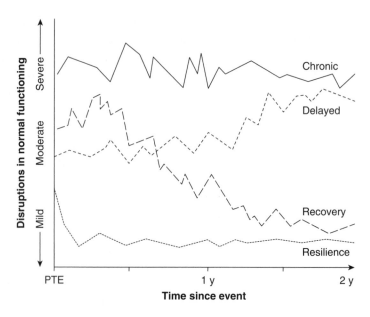

Figure 5.2 Four possible emotional trajectories following a potentially traumatic event (Bonanno, 2004)

has the ability to thrive even in the face of extreme adversity, and that a resilient response to a potentially traumatic event is a common response from the majority of people exposed to trauma.

Such a perspective may be encouraging in terms of future positive outcomes for the majority of children exposed to traumatic events, but it also illustrates the complexity of the issues, as Bonanno and Mancini (2008) point out in this caveat:

> [T]hat evidence for resilience in children typically requires more careful and elaborate monitoring across multiple domains (e.g. peer relations, school performance). (p. 371)

Bonanno (2004) has outlined four different trajectories following a potentially traumatic event: *chronic, delayed, recovery* and *resilience* (see Figure 5.2). Our work in the adaptive emotional development component of the 'Authentic Warmth' approach to childcare relates specifically to the recovery trajectory. The prolonged disruption in normal functioning that often occurs in either the delayed or the chronic trajectories, will require a more detailed investigation, more powerful strategies which address the complexity of the child's responses and longer-term intervention. On the other hand, children and young people whose responses to trauma fall into the resilience trajectory (possibly a majority?) are likely to do well in placements which provide authoritative parenting, build on their strengths and encourage these children and young people to make the most of educational opportunities.

An important role for the psychologist consultant is to monitor the trajectories of each child to ensure that chronic reactions are identified and that those responsible for the child's placement are alerted so that the importance of the work with the child or young person is understood and that the authority continues to track and support progress. As Figure 5.2 also indicates, regular reviews of children in the recovery trajectory are also essential to check the possibility of a delayed reaction occurring.

For policy-makers and commissioners of social care for children, Figure 5.2 also illustrates a poorly understood, but particularly important, feature of professional childcare for unhappy children, namely, a typical recovery period of one to two years. While courts are compelled to adhere to legislation, which requires primary consideration to be given to the needs of the child, it is readily recognised that local authorities, which are often faced with financial constraints may be forced to prioritise *many* primary considerations. These pressures can lead to the poor, or even damaging, practice where it is not uncommon for local authorities to change a child's placement, often in the face of opposition from the child's social worker, without consulting the child or young person, and at short notice. We return to this topic in Chapter 9 when we invite everyone within the corporate parenting circle to examine how they discharge their civic responsibilities.

Post-traumatic Growth

The concept of growth following suffering can be found in many ancient cultures and religions (see Tedeschi and Calhoun, 1995) but appears to have been overlooked to a surprising extent in the more recent history of psychology. Since the First World War, applied psychologists have concentrated on helping people to cope with the adverse reactions to grief and trauma, and to focus on alleviating mental illness; the idea that emotional growth could follow adversity was largely ignored or only mentioned as an interesting side issue. It is only relatively recently that empirical studies have begun to embrace ancient wisdom and to rediscover the potential of helping clients to work beyond coping, encourage emotional growth and enable individuals to report 'important changes in perception of self, philosophy of life, and relationships with others in the aftermath of events that are considered traumatic in the extreme' (Tedeschi, 1999, pp. 320–1).

Over the past 10 years, increasing attention has been paid to this fascinating phenomenon (see Joseph and Linley, 2008; Linley, 2000; Tedeschi and Calhoun, 1995; 2004). These researchers view the post-trauma stress which occurs either as a result of a single seismic event in that person's life or the prolonged exposure to dramatic events as a continuum of adaptive behaviour rather than an abnormal reaction and, providing they can work their way through the resulting stress, there is a real possibility of positive change and growth taking place in their lives. Many of these growth features link with the research literature on resilience and well-being since the 'growth' dimension of post-traumatic stress can lead to an appreciation of personal strength, the development of compassion and empathy for others and a heightened awareness of events in everyday life.

Applied to the challenge of supporting traumatised children in public care through recovery, Joseph and Linley (2008) argue that the cognitive–emotional processing by a child that follows traumatic events, is likely to achieve any of three possible outcomes:

1   *Assimilation*: the new trauma-related information is absorbed into existing beliefs and models about the world, for example, a self-blame strategy would lead to the unhelpful belief that 'I probably got what I deserved'. This unhelpful and self-limiting view of the world often involves the child defensively maintaining beliefs in spite of evidence to the contrary.
2   *Negative accommodation*: this involves a revision and change in beliefs and models of the world to 'accommodate' trauma-related information. However, if (as is the case for many children in public care), the environment is not supportive and the young person has low expectations with regard to autonomy, competence and relationships, these factors are likely to lead to a 'negative accommodation' with depressive, hopeless and helpless views of the world predominating.
3   *Positive accommodation*: like negative accommodation, this involves a change in beliefs about the world to 'accommodate' trauma-related information; the significant difference being that growth will only occur with 'positive accommodation'. For this more functional view of the world, what is needed is an environment which supports the young person in a positive way by encouraging close relationships, autonomy, positive self-perception, emotional competence, a sense of belonging, indeed all of the eight Pillars of Parenting detailed in Chapter 3. With such growth comes an appreciation of life, the valuing of relationships and the ability to live in the moment (instead of pinning all hopes on a miraculously changed and totally different future).

In their everyday encounters with children and young people who are working towards adaptive emotional development, this process of positive accommodation can be aided by the following carer-support activities:

- helping children to understand where some of their powerful emotions originate
- helping them build their faith and trust in other people
- helping children to avoid blaming themselves for some of the failings of their parents
- enabling them to manage self-doubt and to set high aspirations
- setting boundaries and helping children to work towards self-management of their learning and behaviour and self-determination

- depersonalising negative experiences; for example 'Mum moved out because she and Dad just couldn't get on/just couldn't put up with Dad's violent behaviour any more' versus 'Mum moved out because she didn't love me any more'
- self-management; for example, 'I tried to calm down by talking to myself, phoning up my mate, Chris, or going for a walk in the park'
- helping children to see some of the 'good things' that happen in life and some of the kindness and thoughtfulness that other people show
- helping children to recognise 'good days' and some achievements.

A paradigm shift away from the current, problem-focused treatment position on post-traumatic stress has been proposed by Joseph and Linley (2008) who have argued that 'it is possible that existing therapies for trauma may sometimes thwart growth-related processes' (p. 15). Their professional position, based on 'organismic valuing theory' posits an intrinsic motivation toward growth, i.e. 'people are motivated to pursue positive accommodations following trauma, just as they are through life in general' (ibid., p. 15).

Growth from adversity may offer an alternative explanation to the now well-known study by Jackson and Martin (1998) in which they traced a small group of people who had grown up in care and had gone on to achieve educational success. The study used a risk and resilience framework and identified being able to read at an early age and success in education as crucial factors in their more positive life trajectories; however, the fact that these children and young people had been 'in care' confirms that they endured separation from their parents. In a broader study, which also looked at successful life trajectories, Eisenstadt (1978) proposed a theory which attributed eminence and genius to a child's reaction to the death of one or both of their parents. Eisenstadt used listings from both the *Encyclopaedia Britannica* and the *Encyclopaedia Americana* to identify 699 individuals who had achieved occupational eminence in their life. He then looked at information about their age at the time of the death of one, then the other parent and concluded that 'genius or eminence appears to be related to orphanhood factors' (Eisenstadt, 1978, p. 216).

So, the common theme of growth following adversity runs through Joseph and Linley's 'organismic valuing theory', Jackson and Martin's 'high achievers' and Eisenstadt's 'geniuses'. Although the effort involved in supporting children who have had major negative experiences in their lives is huge, for adults working in childcare, the practice implications of the growth-through-adversity potential for children in public care is both professionally promising and personally motivating. With skilled support from carers, and thoughtful guidance from a psychologist consultant, strategies for work with young people can be designed so that carers can not only support children's positive accommodation to emotional trauma, but also their positive future life development.

Concluding Comments

Although it may not be a novel perspective of the plight of children and young people in public care, once again it has become clear that we need to begin to tackle their emotional problems before we can expect them to achieve great academic gains. Carer support for adaptive emotional development through the 'Authentic Warmth' model of childcare does not mean helping children and young people to forget or dismiss dramatic events, but rather involves enabling them to process negative experiences and helping them to fit such experiences into a place among the other life experiences (both positive and negative).

The support needed to achieve this growth is as varied and unique as the number of children and their individual differences, but pulling together all the components of the 'Authentic Warmth' approach offers carers a coherent theoretical explanation of *what* to do, *why* to do it and *what not* to do. It can also provide carers with concepts and the confidence to challenge ill-informed decisions, to champion the rights of children in their care and, most importantly, to be the catalyst for the child to start on an upward spiral in terms of their life trajectory.

The importance of this reconstruction process is that it can begin to equip children and young people to deal not only with the challenges, but also the possibilities of an independent adult life. The search for meaning and emotional adaptation may not be an easy one, but there is now evidence to suggest that it is not in vain and that at the end of this process, there is a likelihood of becoming a more complex and emotionally stronger individual.

Time for Reflection

If the right kind of emotional support can lead to post-trauma *growth*, are we setting unrealistically *low* targets when we aim at 'enabling children and young people to cope' in an adult world?

6
The Education Dimension

I've come to the frightening conclusion that I am the decisive element in the classroom. It's my personal approach that creates the climate. It's my daily mood that makes the weather. As a teacher, I possess tremendous power to make a student's life miserable or joyous. I can be a tool of torture or an instrument of inspiration. I can humiliate or humor, hurt or heal. In all situations, it is my response that decides whether a crisis will be escalated or de-escalated and a student humanized or de-humanized.
          (Haim G. Ginott, 1922–73, teacher, child psychologist and psychotherapist)

Having made a strong argument concerning central government's overemphasis on increasing the educational attainments of looked-after children in the first two chapters of this book and having followed this with an equally powerful plea for an overdue recognition of the importance of meeting the parenting needs of children and young people in public care and supporting their adaptive emotional development, it may seem paradoxical to be devoting an entire chapter to the 'education dimension' of childcare. However, it would be a major oversight to ignore the potential power of the educational process to enhance (or sometimes constrain) the personal, social, academic and economic outcomes of all children, but particularly those who are in public care. Conversely, we readily recognise that educational underachievement too often reduces life opportunities, can lead to social exclusion, limits their employment prospects and encourages a drift towards a parallel world of alcohol and substance abuse, sexual exploitation and crime.

Of course, the educational system not only provides opportunities for achieving academic outcomes, it is also a powerful force for fostering personal and social development. Hart et al. (1996) have noted some of the subtle dynamics of the educational process, when they claimed that school and college personnel were likely to be among the most reliable sources of compensatory relationships and role models for children who otherwise did not have good relationships or who did not have positive adults in their lives. Further, schools were 'therapeutic environments' in that they promoted achievement and the attainment of pro-social development in children, even when mental health problems and family pathology were present. In his review of education and residential care, Kendrick (1998) mentioned two important, but often overlooked, benefits of a positive educational experience: building up powerful resilience factors in the life of a child, and acting as a source of stability when everything else in the child's life was uncertain.

The power of education as a force for positive change in the lives of young people has also been highlighted by Jackson and McParlin (2006) who wrote that 'each step of the educational ladder is associated with improvements in health, employment, income, housing, family life, the absence of addiction problems and lower risk of involvement with the criminal justice system' (p. 90).

> A high quality education provides the foundation for transforming the lives of children in care. Those who do well in education are more likely to go on to employment, to lead healthier lives and to play a more active part in society. (DfES, 2007, p. 9)

The Attainments of Children and Young People in Care

By now, readers will be only too familiar with the year-after-year information, which reiterates the poor examination results obtained by children and young people in public care. Of the 6,000-plus teenagers who leave care each year, about 60 are likely to go on to university or further education (Sergeant, 2006), a dismally small figure which contrasts sharply with the 43 per cent of the population as a whole who are currently in the higher education sector.

The Department for Children, Schools and families (DCSF, 2008a) report on attainment outcome indicators for looked-after children did not present evidence likely to lead to future optimism; in fact, their statistics indicated that the gap in examination results between children in public care and their peers had actually *increased* and the following disappointing outcomes were reported:

- Compared with 62 per cent of all children and young people, only 13 per cent of young people in public care obtained five good GCSEs (grades A–C).
- Twenty-eight per cent of the looked-after population had Statements of Special Educational Needs and this contrasted with just under 3 per cent of all children and young people in England.
- More than one in seven looked-after children had missed at least 25 days of schooling and one in a hundred had been permanently excluded from school (DCSF, (2008b) data estimate the number of permanent exclusions in England for all children to be 0.2 per cent).
- At age 16 almost a third of young people in state care had not sat a single GCSE or GNVQ examination (in contrast to approximately 1 per cent of the general population).

Table 6.1   Some of the tensions which exist in the education system today

- The desire to support vulnerable pupils versus the demands for higher attainment outcomes
- The needs of the individual pupil versus the needs of the school population as a whole
- Equal opportunities versus the quest for excellence
- Enhanced choice for pupils in general versus diverting school resources to support disadvantaged groups (including children and young people in public care)
- Inclusion versus special classes/curricula
- Entitlement versus resource management expectations

Important Central Government Initiatives

A complete chapter of the DfES (2006) publication *Care Matters: Transforming the Lives of Children and Young People in Care* is devoted to providing a 'first-class education' for this client group, where it is recognised that, because of the trauma and other difficulties they bring with them they 'approach education at a disadvantage'. To combat such negative antecedents, a number of important improvements for the children in care population are mooted, including: providing local authorities with the power to direct schools to admit those in care (even when the school is fully subscribed); creating a general assumption that children and young people in care should not move schools in Years 10 and 11 (unless it is clearly in their best interests); offering free entitlement to school transport to allow looked-after children to remain in the same school after a placement move; providing funding which should enable schools to offer an 'excellent personalised education' to children in the care of the local authority; creating 'virtual' head teachers to support schools in their work with children in care; providing mandatory training for new principals in further education colleges; and setting up pre-apprenticeship training to help young people gain the skills needed to succeed in an apprenticeship scheme.

Despite their obvious potential for support, all of the above tasks join a long list of requirements and priorities which schools are being asked to take on in today's society. Often it is possible to incorporate such improvements into existing school practices, but frequently many of these demands would appear to compete with one another and produce tensions within both the education and school systems. As a backcloth to this chapter on the education dimension some of these tensions are listed in Table 6.1.

So What Is Missing?

Raising the educational attainment outcomes of children in care which lag so far behind those of the general population clearly needs to begin with early intervention that can avert domestic violence, eliminate the effects of poverty on families, build up positive parenting skills and prevent young people from entering the care system in the first place.

What do young children require to promote positive cognitive development and good attitude towards learning? The Ramey Partnership at the University of Alabama at Birmingham, who are major proponents of early intervention, have carried out research over two decades which has enabled them to highlight the following key parental tasks: encouragement to explore, mentoring in early skills, celebration of achievement, rehearsal and extension of new skills, protection from inappropriate disapproval, and a rich and responsive learning environment (Ramey and Ramey, 1998).

Unfortunately, the majority of children and young people who enter the care system have had a history of rejection, abuse and neglect, so early intervention is not an option at this late stage. In addition, they are likely to be educationally well behind others of the same age and are going to require additional help and support in the classroom, both of which are often recognised as Harker et al. (2003) discovered when they ascertained the children's perceptions of useful and less useful support in school.

The reality for many young people in care is that education is the last thing on their minds: survival is their priority and for them the world is an unfriendly place. It is only when these children are helped through these emotional problems, begin to feel good about themselves, develop a sense of belonging and can have fun that the world becomes an interesting place, full of opportunities – a place to explore. In this new state of mind, children who have been rejected, neglected and abused become able and willing to take advantage of educational opportunities.

Within the context of the children in public care, it is worth reiterating the statement by Howe (2005):

> The more secure children feel, the more time, energy and inclination they have to seek understanding and make sense. Whereas fear constricts, safety expands the range of exploration. This is why the social, emotional and cognitive development of abused and neglected children is so heavily compromised. They don't feel safe; they rarely relax. Fear for these children can be so endemic that exploration is weak, anxious and sporadic. (p. 3)

Despite their disadvantages, however, there is survey evidence which indicates that the majority of children and young people in public care hope to do well at school.

> Children and young people in care tell us that they want to lead normal lives. They want to succeed in education, enjoy a wide range of positive activities

and make a successful transition to adult life. We must help them to reach their potential by providing excellent parenting, a high-quality education, an opportunity to develop their talents and skills and affect the support for their transition to adulthood. (DfES, 2007, p. 5)

What Supports Educational Success?

For the past decade or more, researchers have attempted to identify some of the features of the care and education system that appear to reduce the academic opportunities of children and young people who are looked after. Jackson and McParlin (2006) have singled out some of the more obvious constraints including: the low priority given by some social workers to educational matters; disrupted schooling due to frequent placement changes; the likely lowered expectations of teachers and social workers; the well-documented literacy problems of children in public care; poor access to educational books and conducive conditions for study (especially in residential care); and the often low educational levels of carers (p. 92).

The Jackson and Martin (1998) study focused on the minority of high-achieving young people in the care system and identified the following attainment-enhancing factors, all of which clearly need to go on to the support agendas of all local authorities: stability and continuity in education; learning to read early and fluently; having a parent or carer who valued education as a route to a better life; having friends are who are doing well at school; developing out-of-school interests and hobbies; meeting a significant adult who acted as a consistent mentor or role model, and attending school regularly (p. 578).

Disruptive Behaviour in the Classroom

As already mentioned, children who have gone through major traumas and life-changing experiences are unlikely to be able to come into school, sit down, open their books and get on with their class work. Often the disruptive behaviour that they exhibit can be interpreted as a direct, and personal, challenge to a class or subject teacher's authority and can result in the development of a vicious circle where it becomes more difficult for a teacher to maintain a professional attitude to the behaviour and to display more flexibility and tolerance towards the child concerned. Paradoxically, the authoritarian management by the teacher may result in yet more disruptive behaviour from the child or young person who may interpret the teacher's tougher response as 'unfair' and 'personal'.

A helpful publication by Ofsted (2005) entitled *Managing Challenging Behaviour* offers some suggestions on how schools as organisations and local authorities can support improved teaching, an appropriate curriculum for engaging more difficult pupils and consistency among staff when meeting the special needs of children in care. However, the professional challenge of having a difficult to manage pupil in the classroom remains and is likely to require more than the indirect influences of organisational change; providing the teacher with the knowledge and skills to change pupil behaviour becomes a priority task for the applied psychologist.

Miller (2003) has argued that there is a strong tendency for people to make attributions about complex events, like difficult classroom behaviour. The most frequently employed causal attributions of teachers, parents and pupils to emerge from Miller's studies can be summarised as follows:

- Teachers attribute pupils' difficult behaviour mainly to the *children themselves* (for example, need for praise, non-acceptance of social norms, physical/medical problems, and so on) or to *adverse home factors* (for example, parental management of child, violence in the home, and so on).
- Parents attribute pupils' difficult behaviour to *unfairness of teachers' actions* (for example, picking on a particular pupils, blaming unfairly and not listening) and *pupil vulnerability* (for example, peer influences and adverse home factors).
- Pupils attribute other pupils' difficult behaviour *to unfairness of teachers' actions and pupil vulnerability* (ibid., 143).

The important point that Miller went on to make about these different explanations offered for the behaviour of children and young people in school was that of their perceived controllability. If teachers view difficult and challenging behaviour as being within the child's control, then they are more likely to be sympathetic to the child's needs, more tolerant and more supportive to the child. So, helping teachers to see more clearly what underpins such behaviour by children in public care becomes a particularly important task for supporting professionals like psychologists.

Obviously, sharing the deeper knowledge of the negative effects of rejection, abuse and neglect (discussed in Chapter 2) will be a good starting point for increasing teacher awareness and with this end in mind, the National Children's Bureau has produced a helpful booklet for teachers to enable them to understand the process of attachment and how secure and insecure attachment can affect the education of all children, particularly those who are in public care (Ryan, 2006). Similarly, teachers need to know that dysfunctional early relationships are also of central importance in the neuronal growth of prefrontal executive functions, which include memory, narrative, emotion representation and states of mind, all of which, as Greig et al. (2008) have pointed out, are crucial for scholastic achievement and social adjustment.

Table 6.2 Pupil behaviours which might alert teachers to the existence of the more subtle emotional needs of the child or young person

- Incessant chattering
- Low-level but persistent and defiant behaviour
- A lack of respect for people in authority
- The use of 'rights' as a weapon for controlling adults' behaviour
- Low motivation to learn
- An expectation that learning should always be easy and effortless
- An inability to deal with failure

Therefore, children and young people in public care may not only be lagging behind in their education because they have missed days at school or have been too emotionally upset to concentrate on their class work, but they may also have an uneven profile of cognitive abilities which make learning more difficult for them.

More pragmatically, the model of behaviour management offered by Dreikurs et al. (1982) which has been discussed in Chapter 4 and in Cameron, (1998) can enable teachers to look underneath the overt behaviour, to consider the underlying message which the child or young person is conveying through such behaviour and to respond with a more empathetic management approach (see Table 6.2).

Ensuring that teachers have a deeper understanding of the relationship between negative early experiences, the resulting emotional pain and confusion, the challenge of the classroom context and their links with disruptive behaviour, does not absolve the pupil from his or her responsibilities. Carers also need to support the rights of teachers to teach, the rights of students to learn, everyone's right to physical and psychological safety, and everyone's right to be treated with dignity and respect (cf. Hook and Vass, 2004). An example of such support appears in the extract from a consultation session in Illustration 6.1.

As discussed earlier, the educational performance of young people in residential care is often poor and while a likely antecedent is the significant factor that relates to rejection, abuse, neglect and other negative pre-care experiences, other factors implicated are likely to be due to the low expectations of carers, a lack of educational continuity, and minimal home–school information sharing and joint planning. All of these often unintentional constraints have important implications for improving and filling existing gaps in the education and social care systems.

Residential and foster carers need to be alerted to the value of education in providing children and young people in public care with much needed opportunities to experience success, to build up self-worth and to increase their life choices and opportunities. (See Gallagher et al., 2004, for their outline of good practice in the education of children in residential care.)

Illustration 6.1   Notes on a staff consultation session on teaching arrangements for Jono

These notes do not refer to one specific young person but are a composite made up from notes on several children.

The problem: Care staff who accompany Jono to his one-hour home tuition sessions with Ms Smith each day reported his behaviour is particularly disruptive during this session and that he is unreasonably rude to Ms Smith.

Likely contributing factors: difficulties in sitting still, limited concentration, general learning difficulties, the effects of a role model of a violent older brother in his previous home environment and anger at being separated from his three brothers and Gnasher, his dog.

Agreed staff action for managing this problem

1. *Reviewing the Jono/Ms Smith relationship*
   Arthur, Jono's key worker, will have a discussion with Ms Smith which includes the following reflective questions:

   - How do you think the current teaching sessions with Jono are going?
   - What are some of the things that seem to be going well?
   - What are some of the things that are not going well?
   - What important elements are missing from these teaching sessions?
   - How can the carers be more supportive to you and Jono?

2. *Agreeing a new format for these one-hour sessions*
   In order to manage Jono's relatively short, on-task behaviour, the following pattern for a one-hour session in the classroom might be more appropriate:

   - A five minute settling-in period.
   - A 15 minute session of sustained and mentored school work.
   - A five minute session talking about the work Jono has completed and how easy or difficult he had found it.
   - A short break which could include an activity (e.g. a board game) in which the attending care staff member could join.
   - Another 15 minute mentored work period and review.
   - A short 'good ending' including a 'looking-forward-to-tomorrow's session'.

   Arthur (Jono's key worker) will draw up an incentive plan for Jono and try to involve Jono in the design/preparation of his plan.
   As far as possible, one or two members of staff should be consistently allocated to accompany Jono at his home tuition session.

3. *Sharing tuition sessions with another child*

   - Considering the possibility of arranging a short, shared period between Jono and Sally (who also receives home tuition in the next-door room).
   - Jono's key worker will try to align some of the work which is going on at the afternoon school session which Jono attends and the morning home tuition session.
   - Displaying some of Jono's best work in the dining room.

4. *Setting out expectations for behaviour in class*
   Arthur will choose an appropriate moment to talk to Jono about his behaviour in Ms Smith's class, her right to be treated politely and the fact that, although he may have difficulty in realising this, she was keen on helping him and was not going to give up teaching him because she considered helping him to learn was too important for Jono when he becomes an adult, to allow him to stop her from teaching.

Building up Resilience

So far the focus has been on improving the beliefs, attitudes and aspirations of teachers and carers to enable them to understand and manage the disruptive, anti-social, sometimes aggressive and occasionally violent behaviour of children and young people in public care. There is, however, an additional and underestimated component of the educational dimension, namely, its contribution to the development of self-worth, well-being and social competence.

In Chapter 4, we discussed the importance of resilience as a powerful influence in people's lives. High levels of resilience can enable people not just to tolerate life's adversities, but to cope with and to manage these: while vulnerability can be viewed as an individual's susceptibility to being emotionally floored by negative experiences, resilience is their ability to get back up, brush themselves down and start all over again! There is little doubt that what happens in the classroom and in the wider school environment can make a major contribution to the development of resilience in children and young people. Indeed, after the family environment, schools are probably the second most effective environments for building up independence skills, promoting self-efficacy and developing the problem-solving skills of children and young people, especially those who have experienced negative life events. (See Dent and Cameron, 2003, for a discussion of the contribution of educational psychology to the enhancement of resilience in looked-after children and Table 6.3 for some low-energy strategies that teachers have suggested could create a school environment, which is more pupil-friendly, valuing and resilience-enhancing.) In both these areas, there can be an important role for the learning support assistant, as Burton (2008) has described in his indirect but important all-round development activities.

For groups of vulnerable or at-risk children and young people, the *Bounce Back* programme (McGrath and Noble, 2003) is a good example of a curriculum-based

Table 6.3 Some examples of small, but important, resilience-enhancing changes which could be introduced into the school or classroom

- After-school homework clubs
- Encouraging friendships between vulnerable children and successfull peers
- Noting and encouraging the development of talents and natural skills, e.g. sketching, singing, dancing, dramatic skills, games ability, hobbies, interests, etc.
- Enabling the child or young person to develop strategies for effectively managing potential flashpoints like bullying and name calling, attracting a teacher's attention, apologising, saying 'no' assertively, praising other pupils' work, avoiding being labelled 'a boff', etc.
- Giving feedback in the ratio of three positive comments to one improvement suggestion
- Asking children to reflect upon the skills and knowledge they employed when they have successfully completed a classroom or homework task
- Giving praise unobtrusively (especially in the case of secondary-aged pupils!)

approach to teaching resilience and well-being, which has psychological underpinnings and which concentrates on those personal skills and values of resilience that can be taught, namely:

- pro-social values such as co-operation, fairness, support and concern for others
- optimistic thinking, including the use of humour as a coping tool
- helpful thinking
- the skills that lead to goal achievement, including planning, organising, self-discipline, self-reflection and problem-solving
- skills for understanding and managing emotions
- social skills.

It is interesting to note that self-discipline appears to be a particularly important resilience factor and it as been argued that this factor may predict future academic success more effectively than cognitive ability (cf. Duckworth and Seligman, 2005). Such examples of self-discipline include children's ability to follow rules, avoid impulsive actions and the receipt of instant rewards for later gratification.

Some Subtle Possibilities for Support

In large organisations like schools, it is often difficult to create the *sense of belonging* needed to help pupils to identify with the school (Goodenow, 1993; McNeeley et al., 2002), yet this is an important dimension of school life for all pupils and particularly important for children and young people in public care who may never have felt a sense of belonging to any group or organisation. A sense of belonging is an essential human need, yet many children and young people today appear to have little sense of belonging either to place, community or the country in which they live and can often veer towards cliques or gangs which can meet these needs.

> Increasing evidence shows that when adolescents feel cared for by people at their school and feel like a part of their schools, they are less likely to use substances, engage in violence, or initiate sexual activity at an early age. (McNeely et al., 2002, p. 138)

McLaughlin (2007) has studied school-belonging from the students' perspective and come up with the following characteristics:

- feeling valued as individuals
- feeling accepted and included
- experiencing a sense of personal achievement
- feeling involved and listened to
- experiencing meaningful teaching and learning

- understanding and identifying with the school as an organisation (the congruence factor)
- having a sense of personal efficacy, that is, that things are developing for the better.

These factors, which are likely to make young people identify more closely with the school as an organisation and subscribe more readily to the intentions and aspirations of the school staff, could provide an agenda for the organisational change which could not only create an exciting and learner-friendly social environment for students, but also help to build the kind of student–teacher relationships which are fulfilling for both groups.

While negative teacher attitudes to some looked-after children and young people may be understandable, they not only lower the teacher's expectations of good behaviour, but are also likely to obscure the child's talents and assets. Seligman (2002) believes that each person possesses several *signature strengths*, which are strength of character that a person self-consciously owns, celebrates and (if he or she can) incorporates into such daily activities as 'work, love, play, relationships and parenting'. Although originally designed with adults in mind, a 'Children's Strengths Survey' has been produced by Katherine Dahlsgaard, one of Seligman's research colleagues (see Seligman, 2002, pp. 231–44).

The full list of signature strengths (which includes obvious contenders like a love of learning, fairness, humour and enthusiasm) can be found in Seligman's book, but some of the less obvious ones, which may apply particularly to children in public care include the following:

- *Curiosity and interest in the world*. Curiosity about the world entails openness to experience and flexibility about matters, which do not always fit one's pre-conceptions. Curious people do not simply tolerate ambiguity; they like it and are intrigued by it.
- *Practical thinking.* Thinking things through *and examining them from all sides*.
- *Courage* (this includes both moral courage and psychological courage).
- Integrity and honesty, kindness and generosity, loyalty and teamwork.
- *Discretion* (not saying things impetuously that might be regretted later).
- *Gratitude* (being aware of the good things that happen and never taking them for granted.
- *Spirituality* and a *sense of purpose*.

After an individual has identified and personalised their signature strengths, Seligman's advice on their use is to consider how and in what contexts these can be employed in everyday life. Given young people's ease with information technology it is likely that completing their signature strength questionnaire on-line would be an attraction (at www.authentichappiness.sas.upenn.edu). However, the follow-up discussion is likely to be most effective if it takes place in a discussion between a teacher, a carer and the child or young person him or herself.

While Banks and Woolfson (2008) have reminded us of the importance of teacher expectations, they have also pointed out the powerful influence *of a child's own attributions of success and failure* in school on their academic success and schools: those with fixed, internal and unchangeable attributions (like 'I'll just never be any good at maths') tending to perform more poorly than those with positive attributions. One of the subtle abilities of highly successful teachers is the way in which they can encourage the development of positive, but realistic, attributions for success and their gentle challenging of negative attributions.

Concluding Comments

The Health Education Authority (HEA, 1997) has defined mental health as 'the emotional and spiritual resilience, which allows us to enjoy life and to survive pain, disappointment and sadness. It is a positive sense of well-being and an underlying belief in our own, and others' dignity and worth' (p. 7). In more observable terms, a 'mentally healthy individual' has been described by the Mental Health Foundation (1999) as one who can achieve the following complex life tasks:

- develop emotionally, creatively, intellectually and spirituality; initiate, develop and sustain mutually satisfying personal relationships; face problems, resolve them and learn from them; be confident and assertive; be aware of others and empathise with them
- use and enjoy solitude
- play and have fun
- laugh, both at themselves and at the world.

Our mental health influences how we think, feel, value ourselves, value other people and interrupt what is going on both outside and inside our homes. After the home environment, education is likely to be the second most important influence in supporting the positive development of all children, and for some of the more vulnerable, school can also become a powerful factor in enabling them to achieve these criteria of healthy emotional development.

Time for Reflection

As well as supporting the academic attainments of children and young people, how realistic is it to expect teachers to create a sense of belonging, help children to identify and utilise their signature strengths and challenge their self-limiting attributions for success and failure in school?

7
Psychological Consultation and Support

The purpose of psychology is to give us a completely different idea of the things we know best.

(Paul Valéry, 1871–1945, French poet, essayist and critic)

Both the obvious and the often hidden problems faced by children and young people who have experienced rejection, abuse and neglect, are likely to be multi-layered, difficult to unpick and unlikely to have simple solutions. One of the advantages of the 'Authentic Warmth' model of childcare is that it enables carers and the professional practitioners who support them, to cut through some of the complexity and to produce an action plan which builds on the existing skills of carers, leans heavily on psychology as a knowledge base, is supported by the expertise of a chartered psychologist, and is tailored to identify and build on the child's strengths. Such an action plan is specifically designed to meet the needs of a particular child at a particular point in time.

In preceding chapters, we have seen how the Pillars of Parenting can offer a medium for providing much needed parenting experiences during day-to-day encounters with children, while the Cairns approach to post-trauma stress has highlighted the importance of adopting a long-term view of their journey towards emotional adaptation. The information and agreed action that appears in the action plan can help abused and neglected children to experience positive parenting, to engage with their feelings of hurt, guilt and anger, and begin to find an emotional place for such feelings which allows them to move forward in their emotional development. The combined parenting and emotional support features, described in this book, are two key components of the 'Authentic Warmth' approach to childcare.

To support carers in their everyday encounters with what are often disturbed and disturbing children and to enable these to manage some of their problems, which Schön (1987) has described as 'messy, confused, uninformed and denying easy analysis or a ready-made solution', every child psychology practitioner draws upon a sophisticated, but not always obvious or transparent, theoretical base for his or her advice.

The main aim of this chapter is to describe how the consultant chartered psychologist can help carers to develop a deeper insight into the most likely factors underlying such emotional social and behavioural difficulties, and to consider appropriate and evidence-based approaches to the management of such problems so that carers are better able to support children and young people through difficult and sometimes frightening periods of their emotional development.

In particular, we unpack what is often the impressive selection of knowledge, experience and expertise, which goes into high-quality psychological advice, which may not be recognised by the carers, nor always clearly explained by the psychologist.

The Power of Psychology

A psychological perspective can enable carers, who have everyday, direct contact with the children, to 'get a handle on' a complex problem situation and to consider creative possibilities for change. The applied psychology knowledge base is a rich source of concepts, theories and research, which a skilled child psychology consultant can utilise to tease out those subtle factors that provoke or maintain the problem, and use this information to provide carers with a deeper insight into the nature and possible management of the problem situation. In these ways, psychology can validate, inform and challenge the practice of carers.

> The psychologist adds a distinct perspective, asks particular types of questions and uses validated interventions and tools. This perspective is grounded in scientific psychology on the one hand and a commitment to evidence-based practice and scientific methods on the other. (*EuroPsychT*, 2001, p. 8)

The 'Authentic Warmth' model provides a powerful framework for meeting the needs of children and young people in public care, an integral aspect of which is the facilitation and advice of an applied psychology consultant. This builds on, complements and interprets the detailed intimate knowledge of the child, which the carer will have built up. Integrating the combined knowledge base of the carer and the psychologist with the main components of the model, namely, the employment of the Pillars of Parenting enables the carer to provide positive parenting experiences for the child. The ABC+C of behaviour management, the adaptive emotional support needed for the post-trauma stress and, where possible, the experiences which work in the child's school are the key components of the process known as 'consultation'.

Consultation Is ...

Consultation has been defined in a number of ways in the professional literature. For example, Wagner (2000) views the approach as a 'voluntary collaborative non-supervisory approach established to aid the functioning of a system and as inter-related systems' (p. 11). A more transparent and grounded definition of consultation has been provided by Sheridan and colleagues who perceive the process of consultation as interpersonal actions involving 'an indirect problem-solving process between a [consultant] and one or more [consultees] to address concerns presented by a client' (Sheridan et al., 1996, pp. 341–2). Although this latter definition may not be able to encapsulate consultation in its different guises, it does highlight common components like problem-solving and the triadic relationship between a consultant (for example, a chartered psychologist), a consultee (that is, a parent, carer or teacher) and the child who is the focus of concern (for example, a child in care or a pupil in the classroom). The definition by Sheridan and his colleagues makes explicit mention of the indirect nature of the support from the consultant, which is delivered to the child via the direct contact carer(s) and recognises that the consultation *process*, as well as the *outcome* for consultees and children, are both worthy of regular scrutiny.

The Evidence Base for Consultation

A number of US reviews and meta-analyses of published research, dating back to the 1970s, have investigated the question, 'how effective is consultation?' Like many apparently straightforward questions in psychology, this one also turns out to be deceptive, especially since the involvement of at least three key individuals engaging in complex, interpersonal interactions (see Figure 7.1) means that decisions about what are the most appropriate efficacy factors to measure and how to measure these, are challenges for researchers and practitioners alike (for a discussion of some of these issues, see Kennedy et al., in press).

Despite these complexities, the findings of most reviewers are similar, namely, that conjoint behavioural consultation is effective across a variety of different problem situations and consultation remains a highly promising approach for adapting applied psychology for use in complex problem-solving situation (cf. Knoteh et al., 2003; Reddy et al., 2000; Sheridan et al., 1996; 2001). Expressing the opinions of many authors, Graden (2004) wrote, 'the importance of adopting a model of service delivery based on consultation … that is directed at meeting the needs of children, families and schools … is undisputed' (p. 346).

The Consultation Process

As a result of a dialogue, which builds on the client's personal knowledge of the problem and the knowledge and skill of the consultant, new insights, opportunities and possibilities, are created. These possibilities occur as a result of a marriage between the intimate knowledge of the consultees and the psychological knowledge and professional artistry of the consultant. As its best, such a dialogue creates optimism in both consultee and consultant, builds feelings of control where none previously existed, and promotes positive beliefs that although human problems are never simple, people can improve and develop, and things can change for the better (cf. Miller and Rollnick, 2002).

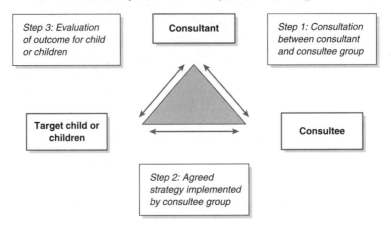

Difficulties, which can have a positive or negative effect on the success or failure of the consultation cycle, can arise at any of these three stages.

Step 3: Evaluation of outcome for child or children

Consultant

Step 1: Consultation between consultant and consultee group

Target child or children

Consultee

Step 2: Agreed strategy implemented by consultee group

Figure 7.1   The key interactions involved in the consultation process

It is not only the problem-solving skills of the chartered psychologist or his or her interpersonal skills (for example, gaining commitment for change), which are unique to this profession: it is the creative application of psychological research and theory which informs decision-making and advice, and which distinguishes the psychologists from others working in the caring professions. This 'professional creativity' is underpinned by the following distinguishing features of applied psychology practice, which are likely to make the chartered psychologist's perspective different from those of other professional groups:

1   Adopting an *interactive perspective* of the nature of human problems. For example problems are most likely to be caused by the interactions between a number of interacting factors that may occur within the child, the family, school or the neighbourhood, rather than having a single source. (For a glimpse of the sophisticated levels of explanations used by the psychologist see Figure 7.2 for a biological, cognitive/affective, behavioural and environmental interactive factors model of vulnerability of children and young people in public care.)

2   Drawing on the knowledge base of psychology to uncover those *mediating or explanatory variables* that may provide an explanation of why certain events may be related (for example, the powerful mediating factor of 'parental rejection' which links a child's early negative experiences with disruptive behaviour in the classroom or in residential or foster settings).

3   Establishing the *key dimensions of human problems.* Using psychology, published research evidence as well as on-the-spot data to provide a simple but practical map of the interaction between people, factors and aspects of their living/learning environments which may be provoking or maintaining the problem(s) under investigation.

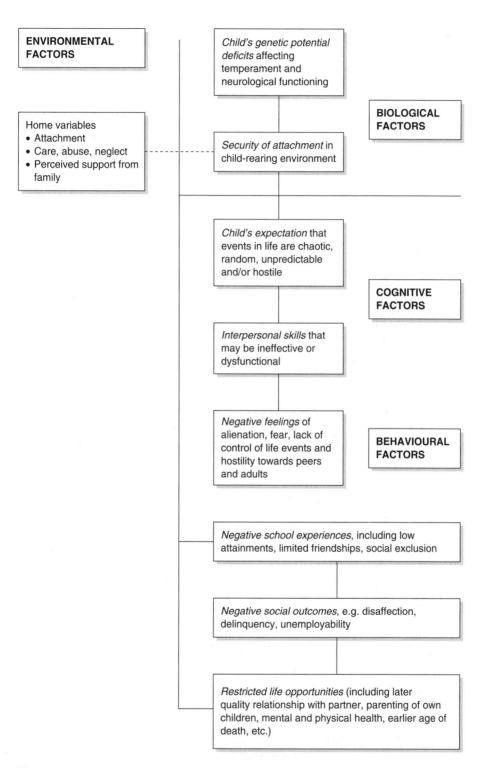

Figure 7.2 An interactive factors model of vulnerability (after Morton and Frith, 1995)

4 Using information from the research and theoretical database in psychology to recommend *evidence-based* strategies for change.
5 Promoting innovative and creative ways of working which are not only underpinned by psychological research evidence and theory, but which can enable clients to spot potential opportunities for positive change.
6 Enabling significant adults, like parents, carers, teachers and others who have direct contact with children and young people, to access, develop and employ a variety of instruments, which can enable them to measure outcomes for children, evaluate their practice and provide evidence, which permits external scrutiny and evaluation of their work.

Essential Consultation Skills

What are some of the professional skills that underlie consultation competence in applied psychology? Although any list that attempts to describe a complex human interaction is likely to be a long one, the key competences are likely to include some of the following:

- *Problem clarification*. Considering different perspectives of the problem, sorting out evidence from hearsay, using semi-structured interview questions, reaching a shared definition of the problem, and so on.
- *Knowledge of the organisation, context and culture* in which residential and foster carers operate. Using research-based information to uncover some of the less obvious organisational features, like contingency planning for emergencies, the beliefs of carers about their work and the nature and level of management support available.
- *Problem analysis*. Generating possible explanations for the problem, checking these out with staff and selecting the most powerful factors for discussion.
- *Managing group decision-making and providing expert advice*. Using skills such as active listening, mutual engagement and turn-taking to work as a problem facilitator in collaboration with consultees (for example, a group of foster or residential carers). Also employing specialist knowledge and experience and offering informed advice when appropriate.
- *Positive re-framing of problems*. Where necessary, helping consultees to move away from commonly held perspectives of problems that mainly stem from internal deficits in the child or young person (and therefore it is difficult to do much about these) to a more context-focused consideration of a child's skills, strengths and other assets, carers' expectations and beliefs, and possible factors in the child's living and learning environment, which may be provoking or maintaining the problem(s).
- *Problem management*. Ensuring that the best possible evidence from the psychology knowledge base guides decision-making and agreed action.

- *Feedback and self-reflection.* Enabling carers to see a transparent connection between psychology and the problem solutions, adopting a constructively critical stance and helping the group to employ a process of self-reflection.

More details of the specific professional skills, which underlie consultation competence in educational and child psychology, can be found in Kennedy et al. (in press).

Consultation and the 'Authentic Warmth' Approach

Regular psychological consultation sessions allow carers to achieve a deeper understanding of the needs of the child and to work jointly with the consultant on providing the best possible support at a particular point in time. The 'Authentic Warmth' model of childcare recognises that as well as selecting appropriate parenting activities from the eight Pillars of Parenting and letting a child see and feel that he or she is cared about, carers also require the training and psychological back-up to enable them to develop a deeper understanding of the emotional and cognitive processes which are taking place while children work through and adapt to the hurtful experiences, which they have experienced.

For residential and foster carers to provide thoughtful childcare practice, an understanding of the process of post-trauma stress becomes essential and this is particularly the case when faced with a child whose behaviour can be perceived as deliberately vindictive and hurtful, and who may frequently reject/spurn/ exploit acts of carer or peer kindness, affection and good intent. (A protocol for consultation within the 'Authentic Warmth' approach to childcare can be found in Figure 7.3.)

From the perspective of a group of carers, the consultation session can be a source of professional valuing where they can have their practice acknowledged, validated or sometimes challenged. When a culture of mutual trust has been built up, both good practice recognition and improvement suggestions are welcomed as consultation encourages the growth of those approaches that will be of most benefit to the child. Indeed, carers have mentioned that during particularly difficult periods in childcare, the input of the psychologist can become a lifeline for those faced on a daily basis with the extreme behaviours that often result from children's painful memories and intrusive thoughts. While sometimes it may be enough for the carers to be able to share their frustrations and anxieties with a sympathetic team and consultant, more often it is the fresh perspectives, alternative explanations, insights and strategies which can give consultation sessions a buzz which inspires, motivates and readjusts the sense of direction.

(1) **Discussing big and modest successes achieved by staff since the last consultation session**   *Around 5 minutes.*

(2) **Providing an update on previous child or young person discussed, including the child or young person's view of progress or otherwise**   *Around 5 minutes.*

(3) **Discussing the management problems of the newly selected child (if any)**

   - Pen portrait of the child or young person
   - Thumbnail outline of the child's problem(s) and discussion of the ABC and +C factors involved
   - Changing key ABC factors and teaching new +C skills
   - Agreed action strategies for management and support
   - Plan for implementation, monitoring and evaluation
   - Summary of agreed action   *Around 15 minutes.*

(4) **Discussing and identifying the child's current parenting needs** (using the 'Pillars of Parenting' list and selecting from the staff-support activities menu)
                                                                Around 5 minutes.

(5) **Discussing and identifying the child's post-trauma emotional needs** (using the Adaptive Emotional Development model and drawing upon the selected items from the carer-support activities menu)   *Around 10 minutes.*

(6) **Discussing the child's assets and talents and considering the learning opportunities, which have arisen from these strengths**   *Around 5 minutes.*

(7) **Summarising and recording the agreed action by carers or consultant**
                                                                Around 5 minutes.

(8) **Carrying out a meta-analysis of the session.** Discussing the process of the consultation session and considering its assets and possible areas for improvement
                                                                Around 5 minutes.

Total time involved = approximately 1 hour

Figure 7.3   Protocol for consultation session with a residential or foster carers' team

Each carer group consultation differs considerably from the more common, traditional psychotherapy session. In an 'Authentic Warmth' consultation session, the focus is on the context in which the child or young person is having difficulties, there is an ongoing dialogue between direct and indirect contact adults, and the main source of support for the child comes from people who are on the spot, rather than from clinic-based therapists (see Dent and Golding, 2006, for a discussion of this issue). Residential and foster carers are ideally placed to carry out this adaptive emotional development work, by providing appropriate advice and positive experiences that can help the process of cognitive reconstruction since frequent and naturally occurring opportunities to provide 'therapeutic experiences' occur during everyday encounters such as when a child or young person seeks reassurance, information, insight or emotional comfort.

As an example of how this works in practice, the notes from a consultation session are reproduced in Illustration 7.1. This contains a summary of the agreed

Illustration 7.1   The notes of a staff consultation session for Ita

These notes do not refer to one specific young person but are a composite made up from notes on several children.

Pillars of Parenting
Living Psychology

Notes from the meeting held at Hogwart's Children's Home

Discussion Session on Ita

Key worker: Chris.

(a) ***Update on child discussed at last consultation session:*** the classroom behaviour management strategy agreed at the last meeting is beginning to work, but Ita still needs a carer in the classroom to prevent her annoying other pupils. The quality of Ita's work has much improved and her new Maths teacher says that she has done well in her end of term test. *Action: review after the Easter break.*

(b) ***Summary of Ita's progress:*** Ita is an attractive and vivacious 13-year-old who has a number of close friends in school and at home. She is empathic towards carers and kind to other children at home, especially the younger ones. Ita's schoolwork is of a high standard, she does her homework without prompting and she is generally regarded as a valued pupil.

   a. ***Problem behaviour:*** sexualised behaviour e.g. flirting, inappropriate dress choice and staring at males inappropriately.

   In general, Ita is doing really well in Hogwart's and at the local school; however, the care staff are becoming increasingly concerned about her sexualised behaviour. Some of Ita's imagined, but vivid, descriptions about her behaviour with her 'boyfriends' and her overt and inappropriate relationship-seeking may be due to immaturity and the role models she experienced in her family. It was mentioned that often the best strategy when dealing with this fantasy behaviour is not to challenge it, but to invite Ita to consider alternative plans for weekends, etc.

   Agreed action for sexualised behaviour – a firm and assertive statement to Ita:

   - 'I think that your choice of clothes is not appropriate for going out. You may feel good about how you look, but other people may see you differently. Let's talk about the messages you are giving out and the ones that you would like to give out.'
   - 'You are making that man feel uncomfortable. Just think for a moment about the messages you are giving out … what do you think that he is thinking about you?'

   It was noted that the staff have been 'up-front and direct' with Ita, when discussing her sexualised behaviour and that in this case, this was an appropriate strategy.

   (Continued)

It was also reiterated that a good rule of thumb for adolescent statements like 'I don't care' was to treat these as bravado/immature/face-saving reactions and not statements of fact ... in other words, staff should persist!

(c) **Ita's parenting needs:** The Pillar of Parenting which was chosen as the priority for eta at this point and to address the most concerning behaviour, namely *Personal and Social Responsibility* is Pillar No.8. Staff action discussed to support this pillar can be summarised as follows:

- Discussing relationships with Ita (work, leisure, sexual, etc.)
- Helping Ita to think about future aspirations

(d) **Working through post-trauma stress**. Some of the abuse experiences in Ita's early background were considered. It was agreed that Ita is moving into the 'Adaptation' phase of the Cairns model. Key staff activities required to promote social connectedness and personal efficacy were agreed to be:

- Reminding Ita about those areas where she can control events in her life.
- Helping Ita to accept some of the life changes which she has experienced.
- The carers at Hogwarts should reiterate the importance of being consistent with her choices, mention the long-term benefits of seeing things through and help Ita to 'hang on in'.
- One task for all staff is to adopt the 'parent role' and to motivate Ita by emphasising that she is maturing and old enough to make decisions.

(e) **Building on signature strengths**.

- Ita has passed all her end of term exams to date and may be able to take her GCSE Geography earlier than the rest of her classmates.
- Ita likes gymnastics and Irish dancing.

One carer will be designated to supervise homework for Ita and two of her peers.

A point to ponder.

A likely issue for Ita could be increasing concerns about body image, due in part to media representations/images of the 'perfect' female shape. Staff reactions to comments such as 'I'm just so fat' should challenge the current 'size zero' obsession.

action for all the main 'Authentic Warmth' components – behaviour management, parenting activities by carers, agreed strategies for supporting the child's adaptive emotional development and activities for helping the child to utilise their strengths. As this summary is a living and working document, which contains the agreed actions by staff and parties incorporated into the individual's care plan, ideally the report should be in the hands of the carers a few hours after the consultation. For the management of the fostering organisation or children's home, two priority tasks are to ensure that (1) the report is available to all carers and (2) the organisational structure is such that it supports the recommended carer activities.

Staff Support

Children and young people will often let us know how they are feeling in a variety of non-verbal ways, often forcefully by evoking powerful and sometimes overwhelming emotions in significant adults, who are trying hard to be supportive. The job of a carer may have its personal rewards, but it is not easy. Not surprisingly, for some time, the conventional view of the residential care sector has been one where carers and managers suffer from low morale and obtain little job satisfaction from looking after other people's children. There is now evidence that this is not an accurate picture and the 'four nations' study quoted in Mainey and Crimmens (2006) has challenged this stereotype by collecting evidence which shows that staff morale and job satisfaction, while not uniformly good across the sector, are better than expected and that there are more aspects of residential childcare practice readily identified as 'positive' than had been evident for many decades.

Importantly too, this study identified those factors which contributed to high levels of personal and professional satisfaction in residential childcare. In particular, it was noted that support from colleagues (as well as managers) and good teamwork not only had a big effect on staff perspectives of their work, but were also critical determinants of the quality of care provided for the children and young people. Mainey and Crimmens also posed challenges for the future, including the establishment of a professional status for carers, a common core of skills and knowledge for the workforce personnel, a clear professional stance, career progression and good leadership and management.

The contribution of carers who are working directly with children, is central to the smooth implementation of the 'Authentic Warmth' model, where the tasks of training, monitoring staff performances and providing high-quality staff support all become organisational priorities. It is recognised that the National Vocational Qualifications (NVQ) Level 3 scheme provides a useful training model involving on-the-job learning and opportunities for demonstrating and discussing core childcare skills with more experienced staff. However, it is clear from our observations that a colleague's advice that is based solely on experience, rather than a carefully researched model of childcare, is not enough to improve practice in professional childcare, so an enhanced curriculum will need to include the following missing topics:

- parental acceptance–rejection theory and its impact on the emotional development of children
- an understanding of the attunement process and its effect on secure attachment
- parenting style and the importance of authoritative parenting on the social development of children
- the processes of emotional trauma, cognitive reconstruction and sensitive support for recovery
- the concept of post-traumatic growth
- the need for continuing professional development for carers and managers, including self-evaluation and reflection.

In this way, the 'Authentic Warmth' model could provide the material for developing good practice in professional childcare, while a modified NVQ could supply the mechanisms for follow-up training and validation. Such a combination could ensure the emergence of carers with sophisticated skills and knowledge, who could not only demonstrate to a child or young person that he or she is cared about (and not just 'looked after') but would also understand and provide appropriate support for the emotional and cognitive processes which are taking place while children work through and adapt to their earlier negative experiences.

Presenting a series of challenges for the future, Mainey and Crimmens (2006) have selected out the following objectives for the childcare professsion – achieving professional status, developing a core curriculum of skills and knowledge, and adopting a clear and well-articulated professional stance – and while ongoing psychological consultation sessions can contribute hugely to achieving these outcomes, there is also a need for continuous professional development so that carers can respond to new challenges in their work and adapt to an ever-changing childcare context.

This means that some consultation sessions are likely to involve professional training and development of carers, rather than having the more common, child-focused format. Topics for these training sessions will arise naturally from consultation sessions and could be *general* issues (for example, using child-valuing language or becoming a high-performance team (see Illustration 7.2) or *child-specific* topics (for example, responding appropriately to children who sexually abuse other children, or who exhibit sexually overt behaviour towards staff, or who self-harm or have eating disorders). Some carer consultation sessions might also include *organisational issues* like adjusting to a new team management, providing good beginnings and good endings for staff joining or leaving, or improving the team (see Illustration 7.3).

The Multi-disciplinary Dimension

Children and young people in care, who have been rejected, neglected and abused are likely to require a variety of specific services, ranging from dentistry to dietary advice. In the case of emotional well-being, where problems are likely to be multi-layered and multi-factorial, professional collaboration is central to the successful support for children and young people who have had major negative experiences in life, yet we would also want to emphasise the distinctive contribution that different groups make. There is an obvious difference between the work of a direct contact residential or foster carer and that of the indirect contact, supporting professions like psychologists, social workers, dentists and others. In this chapter, we have emphasised the distinctive role of the consultant psychologist who is able to draw heavily on the psychology research and theory knowledge base which is the foundation of the 'Authentic Warmth' approach, and while we readily recognise that there will sometimes be a close relationship and some overlapping between disciplines of psychology and social work, there are also distinctive contributions which each professional group brings to discussions and planning meetings.

Illustration 7.2 *Follow-up to a professional development workshop for carers on the requested topic of 'Understanding group dynamics and becoming a high-performance team'*

A summary of the consultation session

Present: The team (seven carers and a senior manager) and the consultant psychologist.

The current situation
Following on from original consultation session in June and the July workshop on 'Understanding group dynamics and becoming a high-performing team' a number of team building and development activities had now taken place, including-

➢ A team night out.
➢ The appointment of two new members of staff who are eager to fit into the team. It is felt that their arrival has helped to readjust the work–life balance difficulties mentioned by team members at an earlier consultation session.
➢ The efforts of the managers to value and recognise high-quality work/extra effort/creativity and innovation by teams and individuals have been welcomed. The recognition that quality work 'on behalf of children', as well as 'with children' is also being recognised.
➢ The growth of a general feeling that enthusiasm and team morale/spirit is slowly moving towards the high level it reached a year ago.

Some future considerations

➢ Efforts by the Director, the management team and all staff to highlight the assets and benefits of a placement for vulnerable children and young people in the two children's homes are generating some positive results.
➢ More leadership input and contact time from the Director, as well as the senior managers, at both a team and at an individual level would be regarded as really valuable and would be welcomed by the team.
➢ Another team night out could be arranged. 'Going to the Dogs' was suggested!!!
➢ Thoughtful and sensitive activities and support to make the new staff identify with the team need to be continued.

Illustration 7.3 *Summary of a consultation session requested by carers on the requested topic of 'Regaining team spirit and well-being'*

Summary of this consultation session

Present: Eight team members and the consultant psychologist.

The current situation

➢ Staff recognise that professional childcare with vulnerable and (often) emotionally damaged children is an occupation which can be physically and emotionally demanding, draining and difficult. They also readily accept that such work can bring the high levels of personal satisfaction, which are missing, in many other public and private sector jobs.
➢ For a variety of reasons, events during the past few months seem to have had a particularly stressful and anxiety-provoking effect on all staff.
➢ While staff feel that all six children living in the home have responded positively to the staff care and warmth (and two of these have made exceptional progress) there is a shared feeling that enthusiasm and team morale/spirit is lower than it was at the same time last year.

(Continued)

(Continued)

> Part of this lower-than-usual team enthusiasm and well-being may stem from the current (and national) reduced demand for residential care places and the possibility of staff redundancies which could result.
> Another factor may be the reduced degrees of flexibility of a smaller work staff which can lead to additional demands on staff time, having to fill in more frequently for sick or unavailable colleagues, feeling obliged to give up part of a non-working weekend when staff availability is tight.
> Within the profession, there appears to be more paperwork and unforgiving deadlines, an increasing number of phone enquiries and more take-home work to complete.
> Additionally, there is a feeling of regret that some of the professionally satisfying activities have been almost squeezed out of the working day. These include: time for thorough handover briefings, critical incident debriefing with a colleague, opportunities to exchange informal views and comments/humour exchange with other team members.
> Finally, staff members would like to work towards restoring the high levels of enthusiasm, energy and personal fulfilment, which the team had reached twelve months ago.

Achieving positive change for the team

1. Strategies already in hand include:

> Interviews for new staff members will be taking place.
> Creative and strategic management of the staff rota to incorporate some personal and family factors, as well as important work demands are being instituted.
> Efforts by the Director, the management team and all staff to highlight the assets and benefits of a children's home placement for some vulnerable children and young people are beginning to get some results.

2. Some possible strategies to consider.

> A staff evening in (or out) to renew informal contact between team members and to savour the team ethos.
> More leadership input and contact from the Director at both team and individual levels.
> An opportunity to reflect with a manager on current personal life–work balance.
> An additional dimension to the management system which values and recognises high-quality work/extra effort/creativity and innovation by teams and individuals. Quality work can take place with the children, but also with colleagues, foster carers, social workers, parents, local government officers, school staff, etc.

Milligan and Stevens (2006, p. 3) emphasised not only the necessity for all-round partnerships, but also the differences between residential workers and social workers, and noted that there are major differences in the work that the different groups do and the skills that they commonly deploy. The recent development of multi-disciplinary children's services in local authorities has encouraged a fashionable view that everyone has important things to say about every aspect of a child's development, yet in our experience it is when psychologists attempt to become amateur social workers (and vice versa) that collaborative practice can turn into confrontational exchanges and professional self-interest. Truly integrated, multi-disciplinary teams not only need to share a common language, but also be prepared to recognise and value, those distinctive perspectives which different professionals bring with them to discussion and planning meetings.

The idea of a named person who acts as a single point of contact for a child and his or her family would seem to make good sense, especially when a range of services is required (cf. Children's Workforce Development Council, 2008). However, co-ordinating services for children (and families) is only one component of the support equation; other important roles include the key worker whose job is to oversee the everyday personal needs of a child and young person in care, while a third level of support is the ongoing support, advice and training required by the carers themselves, which is likely to require an outside staff consultant.

Measurement and Evaluation

As previously mentioned, psychology can inform and challenge the activities of carers by drawing on information from research and practice, but it can also enable them to make changes to existing practice by evaluating the outcomes of their efforts for the children and young people in their care. Of course, there are 'hard data' indicators of change, including a child's acquisition of new skills, an increase or decrease of incidents of unwanted and unsocial behaviour, a reduction or an increase in self-harming behaviour, nightmares or absconding, and improvements or otherwise in school attainment levels; however, none of these give any indications about why these events are occurring.

> Everything that can be counted does not necessarily count: everything that counts cannot necessarily be counted. (Augustine, *De Quanititate Animae*)

When attempting to quantify and understand the effect of the 'Authentic Warmth' model on children and young people, there are a number of commercially produced measures, such as those used by Evert (2007) and set out in Table 7.1. Such measures are useful because they can provide snapshots of a child's development (or lack of development). Some of these measures can be useful to care staff, managers and supporting professionals because they can provide comparative data which can offer an answer to the question 'how does this child's or young person's performance compare with other children of his or her age?'

Although the Evert study was a pilot, which involved the collection and analysis of baseline and post-baseline data over a short (two-month) period, nevertheless, some interesting child outcomes were noted. The first of these was that little or no change occurred in basic skills, well-being and executive functioning, but significant improvement had taken place in emotional areas like depression, dissociative symptoms (including de-realisation, emotional numbing and pretending to be someone else) and sexual concerns subscale. Although these measured improvements in emotional development are promising, larger-scale studies, carried out over a more appropriate period of time of one to two years, are now required to establish the impact of the 'Authentic Warmth' model of childcare.

Table 7.1 List of published tests and measures used by Evert (2007)

Authors	Test	Topic	Done by
Naglieri, J.A. et al. (1993)	Devereux	Problem behaviour	Teacher, carer
Dodge et al. (1985, cited by Frederickson and Graham, 1999)	TOPSS (Taxonomy of Problematic Social Situations for Children)	Social skills: social situations – behaviour	Teacher
Ryff, C. and Essex, M.J. (1992)	Scales of Psychological Well-Being (nine-item scales)	Psychological well-being	Child
Maines, B. and Robinson, G. (1988)	B/G-STEEM	Self-esteem and locus of control	Child
Frederickson, N. and Simmons, E. (in press)	Sense of Belonging Questionnaire	Sense of belonging	Child
Bar-On, R. and Parker, J.D.A. (2000)	BarOn EQ-I: YV(S)	Emotional competence	Child
Briere, J. (1996)	TSCC (Trauma Symptom Checklist for Children)	Post-traumatic stress, anxiety, depression, etc.	Child
Parry, G. (1990)	Attitudes to being helped	Attitudes to being helped	Child
Elliott et al. (1996)	BAS (British Ability Scales)	Basic academic skills: numbers, reading, spelling	Child
Gioia, G.A. et al. (1996)	BRIEF (Behaviour Rating Inventory of Executive Functioning)	Executive functioning	Teacher, carer

Outcomes for children provide the data that not only inform carers of the results of their efforts, but also provide external validation of the success (or lack of success) of any care model. For many of our children, measuring progress could have been a simple task of collecting data on the number of reported or recorded incidents; however, to back up and illuminate these hard data, more sensitive measures are required to look at the process of change in children over a longer period. For this reason, the 'cobweb diagram' for measuring changes on the Pillars of Parenting and also on the 'adaptive emotional development dimension' have been designed (see Figure 7.4). These 'cobweb' diagrams measure and illustrate the child's or young person's response to positive parenting and post-trauma stress support.

The cobweb recording procedure allows carers to assess the progress of a child or young person on a five-point scale (from 'much worse' to 'much improved') on each of the eight Pillars of Parenting. These results can then be plotted on a cobweb diagram, allowing progress to be measured over time. Different colours can be used to provide a visual display of improvements (or deterioration) over a longer period of time. A similar five-point cobweb scale can provide essential information on the different stages of adaptive emotional development. Failure to demonstrate progress can also be picked up for review.

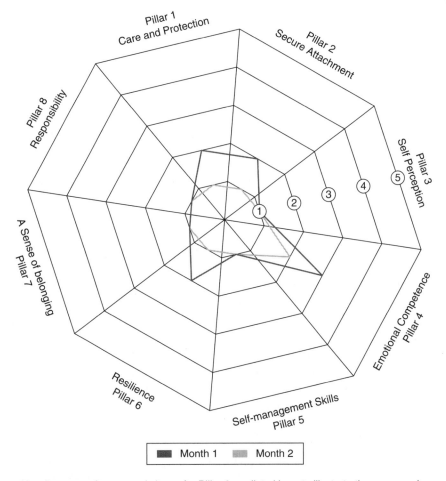

Figure with labels:
Pillar 1 Care and Protection, Pillar 2 Secure Attachment, Pillar 3 Self Perception, Pillar 4 Emotional Competence, Pillar 5 Self-management Skills, Pillar 6 Resilience, Pillar 7 A Sense of belonging, Pillar 8 Responsibility

| ▓▓▓ Month 1 | ▒▒▒ Month 2 |

Key: (because of space, only items for Pillar 3 are listed here to illustrate the measures)
1. Sees self as unimportant.
2. Lack of self-care, with a low perception of self-showing signs of self-neglect or inflated self-perception.
3. Sense of self governed by others.
4. Aware of how others see them and their own ability to change.
5. Awareness of own strengths and weakness with an appropriate positive self-image.

Acknowledgment: Our thanks to our colleague, Andrew Constable, who advised us on the methodology of the cobweb approach to record progress over time.

Figure 7.4 The cobweb record chart for measuring a child's progress (or lack of progress) over time

Such a tool is not only useful for those working directly with the children, as it shows where success has occurred and where future efforts should be directed, but also offers an invaluable, quick-reference visual aid for monitoring officials from the placing authorities. Similarly, the data provided can become an effective monitoring for the placing authority as they provide a visual record of work in progress with the child or young person, as well as areas for future development.

A further possible measure of child progress (or lack of progress) over time is goal attainment scaling. Goal attainment scaling has been described by Lewis et al. (1987) as 'an assessment procedure, which can be targeted to problem areas unique to the individual … while at the same time, yielding numerical values which could be posted for the purposes of comparison between groups' (p. 407). Goal attainment scaling involves the development of goals and indicators with an expected level of outcome for each. The expected levels of outcome are also set for 'somewhat more' (plus one), 'somewhat less' (minus one), 'much more' (plus two) and 'much less' (minus two) (see Frederickson, 2002, for details).

A particular advantage with goal attainment scaling is that the individual scale score can be summed and converted to t-scores using a formula and conversion table provided by Kiresuk et al. (1994) and pooled data of this type can be used to evaluate the effectiveness of different types of support and to examine common factors in the development of groups of children and young people in public care.

The Search Institute in Minneapolis has produced a list of 'developmental assets', which they describe as 'concrete, commonsense, positive experiences and qualities essential to raising successful young people'. During the often difficult transition from childhood to adolescence, these assets have the power during critical adolescent years to influence choices which young people make and to help them to become caring, responsible adults. External examples of these developmental assets include support levels within the family and the community – involvement, empowerment, boundaries and expectations – and internal assets including commitment to learning, positive values, social competence and positive identity (Search Institute, 2007).

As well as changes that occur in the children and young people themselves, another important outcome is the change which can occur in the carers, including in childcare skills, team contributions, carer beliefs and confidence. As well as using checklists with which managers could obtain information on the professional development of staff, another possible approach to measuring staff change would be self-and peer ratings on Baumrind's parenting style model, the three factors under scrutiny here being, *knowledge about and interest in the child*, *expectations for behaviour and learning* and the use of *positive psychological control*. This could be used effectively in supervision as it allows one instrument to measure the quality of the relationship between any given carer and any given child.

Evaluating the Quality of Services and Organisations

In Scotland, HM Inspectorate (education) (2006) produced a framework for evaluating the quality of services and identifying the underpinning factors, which contribute to successful organisations. The particular 'superordinate' questions which are asked in this framework are, *what key outcomes have you achieved, how well do we meet the needs of our stakeholders, how good is our delivery of key processes, how good is our management, how good is our leadership* and *what is our capacity for improvement?* While this represents a useful initial evaluation, general questions like these are not likely to uncover some of the more subtle aspects of an organisation which may be working for or against positive outcomes for staff and children.

'Appreciative Enquiry' is a management procedure which encourages people in an organisation to search for whatever works well (Cooperrider and Whitney, 2000). Although this may seem like a naïve, unworldly and utopian approach to organisational change, this model has a number of surprisingly powerful assumptions, including the need to recognise the healthy parts of the organisation so they can be built up, together with the confidence-building, which occurs when staff can move into a new future taking with them all that has been valuable and functional in the past. These are the principles which underlie the 'Authentic Warmth' Broaden and Build Checklist (see Appendix 1) which focuses on the psychological needs of the child or young person in care with an assumption that basic prerequisites like care and protection have already been investigated in the more traditional inspections carried out by the Office for Standards in Education and are already in place.

The Broaden and Build Checklist is designed to highlight those organisational features of a residential home which would support the 'Authentic Warmth' model of professional childcare and is divided into three main areas of a supportive environment, therapeutic care and the restoration of 'normality' in the lives of looked-after children. These general headings are based on Anglin's (2004) study of the features of successful children's homes.

Concluding Comments

While the Pillars of Parenting offer a medium for providing much needed (and previously missing) parenting experiences during day-to-day encounters with children, the post-trauma adaptive emotional development enables residential staff and foster carers to obtain a deeper understanding of the emotional needs of traumatised children and the importance of adopting a long-term view of the recovery process. Such information can be used to help children to engage with what are often painful, and sometimes shameful, feelings, and to allow abused and neglected children and young people to find a place for such feelings within their current and more positive experiences. These combined parenting and emotional support components can be referred to as 'authentically warm caring' and a comprehensive overview of this professional childcare model can be found in Appendix 2.

Achieving a transparent connection between psychology and the problems of adults and children will require applied practitioners to utilise sophisticated consultation processes and an in-depth knowledge of the discipline, so that they can provide carers with a deeper understanding of problematic situations, offer research-based, creative and effective ways of managing these problems, and promote proactive approaches to minimise the occurrence and impact of such problems in the first place.

Moore (2005) has argued for a continuing, self-critical and reflective stance that examines applied psychology practice within the context of the complexities and changes of contemporary society within the UK. According to Fraser and Greenhaugh (2001) this requires the recognition that as well as *competence* in professional practice, an additional dynamic for professional development has emerged – *capability* – the latter being a characteristic which enables a practitioner to adapt to constant change. The seminal review of consultation effectiveness highlighted that 'well-constructed models (of consultation), articulated from sound theoretical bases may be superior to those without clear conceptual frameworks' (Sheridan et al., 1996, p. 349).

Of course, it must be accepted that pre-care experiences, a variety of within-child factors, the failings of 'corporate parenting' and a lack of appropriate support in school can all become contributory factors in determining outcomes for children and young people in care. However, on their own, none of these can fully explain why so many looked-after children end up with such poor social, educational and personal outcomes. The argument being put forward in this chapter is that authentically warm caring (improving the parenting experiences and the emotional support of children while they are in care), using the knowledge base of psychology and the skills of a consultant psychologist, can not only enhance the well-being of these children but can also lead to improvements in personal, social, academic and economic outcomes. In a nutshell, the challenge for social care is to provide the quality of care and support that is to be found not just in the average family home, but also in the most functional of families.

Time for Reflection

Effective multi-disciplinary work is tantalising, but has proved to be surprisingly elusive: how strong is the case for encouraging the distinctive contributions of each member of a multi-agency or multi-disciplinary team (as well as acknowledging shared practice)?

8
Theory into Practice

In theory there is no difference between theory and practice. But, in practice, there is.
(Jan van de Snepscheut, 1953–94, computer scientist and educator)

Historically, there has been an unspoken belief pervading the childcare profession that looking after children is mainly a matter of common sense. In England, most foster carers do not undergo formal training and it is only since 2001 that residential childcare workers have been required to complete a National Vocational Qualification, Caring for Children and Young People (Level 3), where the focus is mainly on issues like child protection, health and safety, food and hygiene, suitable activities for children and equal opportunities. While the NVQ requirement is a step forward, it is only a tiny one towards a childcare profession with a task-relevant knowledge base and the appropriate skills to understand and support children who have had negative life experiences and to complement their essential personal qualities like sensitivity, empathy and a sense of humour that allows carers to laugh with children (and at themselves).

The outcomes of the Every Child Matters initiative (DfES, 2003) are wide ranging – *be healthy, stay safe, enjoy and achieve, make a positive contribution* and *achieve economic well-being.* They also represent ambitious targets for all children and the significant adults in their lives, but pose particular challenges for those who support children and young people in public care. To work towards these objectives the Children's Workforce Development Council was set up in 2005 to ensure that everyone working with children will have undergone the relevant training and have access to high-quality advice. In their report on the state of the children's social care workforce (CWDC, 2008), improvements in data collection were called for so that the current analysis could be extended to include the future skills and competences which carers will need in order to deliver better services to children. In summary, the report confirmed the need for a workforce that has acquired the relevant knowledge and the practical skills to make a positive impact on the life outcomes of the 60,000-plus children and young people in public care.

'Good practice' in professional childcare involves a complex set of activities, sometimes carried out in trying or extreme circumstances. The good practice links between *what needs to be done* and *how it should be done* are sometimes missing or fractured. In this chapter, the practical issues around implementing the 'Authentic Warmth' approach to professional childcare and the challenges involved in bringing about change within our two children's homes are now considered.

Introducing an innovative model of childcare which would bring about long-term gains for both staff and children, had to take place within the day-to-day running of the children's homes, where carers sought immediate advice and direction, and where troubled children continued to need 'parental' support, understanding, security, boundaries and opportunities.

Background Research on 'Successful' Care

In his study of Canadian residential child and youth care, which was set up to uncover variables which are important to understanding group home life and group home work, Anglin (2002) found that the core variable was congruence to achieve the best interests of the children, that is, the care staff group working together, in agreement to achieve common goals for the young people in their care.

One of Anglin's sobering conclusions was that in a complex organisation like a children's home, congruence can never be fully achieved, since the practical realities and demands mean that achieving common goals can only be an ongoing struggle. He argues that 'rather than demanding the unattainable, perhaps we should heed the recommendation of Winnicott (1986) concerning the aim of achieving "good enough" mothering and "good enough" care' Anglin (2002, p. 65). While such a position might be acceptable as a rule of thumb for on-the-spot assessment of the parenting skills of biological parents by a caring agency, in professional childcare, the children's needs, professional responsibility and the duty of care, demand that not only should 'good enough' parenting be exceeded, but carers should have an understanding of a child's pain and be able to facilitate his or her recovery and, as a result of such nurturance, insight and good practice, to build up a child's confidence, empathy and resilience. For such children, 'good enough' care is just not good enough!

The childcare profession is charged with a singularly important task of changing the (otherwise inevitable) negative outcomes for one of the most disadvantaged groups in our society to those which can lead to meaningful achievement. As such, the profession needs to aspire to greatness, not to remain undervalued and self-deprecating. Most readers would hesitate to allow an operation on a loved one on the recommendation that the brain surgeon is deemed to be 'good enough' or be keen to fly in with an airline which was known to carry out 'it-will-do-OK' aircraft checks. Yet, when we fail to deliver for children in care, not only can the individual end up with reduced life opportunities, but future generations are likely to pay a heavy price in terms of the ensuing cycles of 'damaged' children, adult mental illness, violence and (too often) serious criminal acts.

In a study that highlights the demands on the professional child carer, Clough et al. (2006) have identified three problem categories that can be listed in order of vulnerability and challenge:

1   Children who have relatively simple or straightforward needs.
2   Children (and often families) with deep-rooted, complex or chronic needs.
3   Those children with extensive, complex and enduring needs, compounded by very difficult behaviour.

While a timely intervention which can offer practical advice, with possibly short-term support, may be sufficient to meet the needs of some of the children in the first (and largest) group in our society, for those children and young people in categories 2 and 3, it is only carefully planned and skilfully delivered childcare, of the type which *exceeds* normal good parenting which will be required.

Seeking to identify those factors, which made a difference to outcomes for young people in children's homes, Hicks et al. (2007) carried out a multi-level modelling analysis of data from 30 local authority homes and 15 independent homes. Despite taking in their more problematic children, their report noted that 'the non-statutory sector seemed to do better on a number of outcomes' (ibid., p. 185). While part of the explanation for this finding could lie with the fact that children lived further away from a disadvantaged neighbourhood, the report found that the most significant explanatory variable was *strategy*. 'In homes where the manager had, in our opinion, clear well-worked-out strategies for dealing with behaviour and education, staff had higher morale, felt that they received clear and better guidance, and perceived that the young people behaved better' (ibid., p. 187).

Following their extensive review in *What Works in Residential Child Care*? Clough et al. (2006) also identified three factors from research as being worthy of consideration: *leadership* of a home, *congruity of objectives* between staff in the home, the home manager, external management and wider social systems, and the establishment of *an appropriate culture* within the homes (ibid., p. 81).

In summary, Anglin's exploration of the need to respond to children's pain brings exceptionally skilled childcare into focus, while Clough and colleagues highlighted the necessity of commissioning that is based on the ability to respond to the level of children's needs. (Although children and young people who fall into the Clough et al. category 3 are unlikely to succeed with foster carers, high-frequency breakdowns indicate that many children from this group are still being placed in foster care.) Finally, in the research carried out by Hicks et al. the importance of adopting a strategic approach to professional childcare is heavily underlined.

Regardless of the sophistication of the research methodologies employed, the lack of positive outcomes for children in public care, is less than ideal. When considering these despairing outcomes, the story of a stranger looking for a small isolated village springs to mind: after carefully considering the request for directions, the local responds, 'if I were you, I wouldn't start from here'.

Perhaps a better starting point would be to identify what common universal factors lead to psychologically healthy and happy children, then attempt to uncover the political, organisational and human factors which prevent children in public care from enjoying the fulfilling life that they are entitled to.

Introducing the 'Authentic Warmth' Model

Investigations like those just described may not be able to answer all the big questions relating to high-quality childcare, but they can offer valuable insights and illuminate potential issues relating to the creation of a nurturing, supporting and valuing environment for children who have suffered many negative life experiences. The key factors, which allowed us to introduce and develop our new practice model, can be grouped as follows:

- *A model with a strong psychological knowledge base* supported by regular consultation sessions with a chartered psychologist.
- *Benevolent carers*[1] who were keen to improve their professional knowledge and skills in supporting 'difficult' children and eager to see their efforts making a positive change for the children in their care.
- *Strong and committed leadership.* This involved retaining the strategic/ long-term view, taking necessary risks, thinking creatively and inspiring staff by helping them to see what they and their organisation could become. On a day-by-day basis, a small group of competent, qualified and skilled *managers backed up the new organisational and staff procedures* that were being put into place.

Each of these big factors were influential in the implement of our 'Authentic Warmth' model. The concluding section of this chapter identifies the organisational tasks involved to maintain, monitor, measure and update the new approach', and to ensure that it could adapt to the changing needs of the children and carers. Returning now to our own experience of managing the process of change, we discuss our three key change factors in turn.

1 A Practice Model with a Psychological Knowledge Base

To become a manager in a children's home in the UK requires a social work degree, or an NVQ Level 4 qualification and, depending on location, possibly a course in management. We have always found it difficult to accept that the training required to become the manager of a children's home is so devoid of psychological knowledge, especially since we see this as the most relevant discipline for understanding and helping vulnerable and distressed young people. The main feature of our approach to providing authentically warm childcare for looked-after children and young people is its psychological knowledge base.

Referring back to Clough et al.'s three problems/needs categories, while it is likely that a random training for managers may provide the knowledge to facilitate work with children in the low-demand group (children with relatively simple or straightforward needs) it is less easy to conceive how this background knowledge could be applied to the more challenging problems of children or families with deep-rooted, complex or chronic needs (category 2) or especially the most disturbed and disturbing category 3, children who have extensive, complex and enduring needs compounded by very difficult behaviour. Given the consistently poor outcomes for children and young people in public care, it would not be unfair to claim that the current knowledge base for managers (and carers) falls short of 'good enough'!

The 'Authentic Warmth' approach provides a general framework for good practice, but it needs to be adapted to each individual child's needs. As we saw in the previous chapter, this process is achieved through the consultancy process which involves a child psychologist working directly with the carers and using psychology to provide a deeper insight into the problems and potential of each child and to inform the selection of the particular support strategies tailored to the child's needs. It is the information from the psychology knowledge base adapted in a creative way by the psychologist that enables carers and managers to generate, agree and implement sophisticated strategies in their day-to-day interactions with children. In this way, the 'Authentic Warmth' approach becomes a dynamic model of childcare, as opposed to a static and inflexible one.

The consultant psychologist has a professional remit to include the most recent and relevant knowledge available when addressing the issues and concerns of carers (and managers). Each consultant is supervised by a senior colleague who has considerable experience of working and researching in the social care field, and this pyramid structure has the advantage of ensuring the delivery of high professional standards of consultancy and making sure that carers and managers have access to the most relevant and up-to-date knowledge and practice.

For particularly uncomfortable, unusual or anxiety-provoking issues raised by staff, the expectation would be that the psychologist consultant researches the given issue, tap into the expertise and experience of other consultants, and produce guidelines for staff to enable them to gain a deeper understanding of the issue and to consider which of the evidence-based strategies for reducing or managing the problem are most appropriate for their particular context.

2 Benevolent Carers

To achieve meaningful relationships with children, carers not only need to have good intent and enthusiasm, but also to maintain their role without malice and resentment, sometimes in the most trying circumstances. Smith (2005, p. 3) captured the essential feature of all successful adult–child relationships when he said 'every kid needs at least one adult who is crazy about him (or her)' and observed that 'the most powerful moments in residential child care are when a personal connection is made between a worker and a young person'. While writing this chapter, it struck us that the same could be said about the carers themselves and their need to feel that when the going gets tough, that there is a colleague (for example, a manager or another carer) who has them in mind too!

Smith has also highlighted the 'personal style' of carers and puts this factor into the context of children's homes by discussing the necessity for ongoing 'supervision, debriefing and a culture of openness and dialogue' (2005, p. 3). As we saw in Chapter 2, a concept like 'personal style' can be translated into practice through the use of Baumrind's (1991) model of parenting style: personal style is the individual carer's way of delivering authoritative parenting.

Support which facilitates the relationship between the carer and the child, must come from the top of the organisation, indeed the qualities of benevolence, like warmth; interest and the absence of malice are not only issues for childcare workers; everyone in the organisation, from directors and managers to the part-time cleaners and the visiting handyman, should share the primary goal of facilitating the best interests of the child.

To keep these objectives at the forefront of their work, from time to time, each of these people should ask themselves a few simple but searching questions: *do you see yourself as part of the team, do you help others to get on with their job, what do you do to ensure that the children are treated with dignity, how have you tried to ensure that children are listened to, how have you befriended some of the children, and what would you do if you observed a colleague treating children meanly and unkindly?*

In the case of the latter question, the organisation in which we developed the 'Authentic Warmth' approach to childcare, already had a well-publicised, whistle-blowing policy in place; everyone working in the homes (including the handyman) had received training in child protection and knew exactly what steps to take if they had concerns about how a child was being treated. As well as clarifying what adults should not be doing, the new model enabled managers and carers alike to provide answers to the question we first posed in the opening chapter, 'what would a good parent do?'

It may seem reasonable to assume that people who seek out employment with vulnerable children and young people do so with good intent. Certainly, the majority of carers carry out their work with diligence, kindness and often remarkable patience and skill. However, for those few adults, who choose to abuse their position of power and trust, the full might of the legal system should be used to ensure that children are protected from such malevolent individuals by removing abusers from having contact with children and preventing them from obtaining further work in childcare. The existence of such people blights the profession, devalues the good work and may even reduce the kindness of caring individuals. As mentioned in an earlier chapter, occasional abusive behaviour by a small number of individuals can encourage public paranoia to meet up with overzealous and blinkered political correctness, and can result in draconian legislation and policies, which can constrain the best intentions of benevolent carers to the detriment of the children in their care.

While serious incidents of child abuse are a matter for the police and criminal law and leave no doubt as to the unsuitability of the perpetrator, managers are also faced with the task of addressing an absence of parenting skills or occasional unkindness from carers. Examples of inappropriate childcare practice could include the use of humiliation and guilt to control children's behaviour, a lack of responsiveness and sensitivity to a child, permissiveness (for example, not setting behavioural boundaries) or alternatively strict and inflexible discipline. A good starting point for initiating a discussion about poor childcare practice and encouraging positive change in carers would be an assessment of each carer's parenting style.

On a more positive note, Mainey and Crimmens (2006) set out to identify the future needs of the residential childcare workforce in England, Northern Ireland, Scotland and Wales, and evidence from a cohort of over 1,200 residential childcare workers and found that that 'morale and job satisfaction in residential child care settings is better than much of the conventional wisdom suggested it would be' (p. 85). Their research highlighted the importance of teamwork, leadership, qualification and training but they also acknowledged that 'there is a challenge to create new models of practice to deliver and sustain the changes required by the Every Child Matters agenda (ibid., p. 93).

As part of our 'Authentic Warmth' staff support scheme, we developed our own, more complex version of the parenting style questionnaire, with 10 points on each of three scales: (1) level of control and expectations, (2) level of sensitivity and interest in the child and (3) methods of psychological control. Initially, we offered carers an opportunity to evaluate and reflect upon their own parenting style; however, the questionnaire could not only form the basis of a reflective consultation between an employer and an employee, but could be a useful tool for supervision by ensuring a common team approach to authoritative parenting and also providing a shared language of parenting.

With such a framework in place, the management support task becomes clearer, namely, identifying and changing the (often inadvertent or thoughtless) carer behaviour, which can contribute to an overindulgent, neglectful or authoritarian parenting style. From an employment law perspective, 'unacceptable' behaviour by a carer no longer has to rely on the subjective opinion of the manager, but becomes a transparent act, action or comment which can be evaluated in terms of its impact on the child.

While single examples are unlikely to determine a specific parenting style, this three-dimensional model can allow managers to see patterns of poor childcare emerging and to feel empowered to take action when harmful styles are the dominant pattern. The transparency features of parenting style can produce a powerful protective tool for children, since they provide a sound basis for addressing harmful care practices. Indeed, the transparency of the parenting style questionnaire also facilitates junior care staff in their decision about when to whistle-blow when they see unprofessional behaviour, which may have been overlooked in the past by informal or perceived seniority privileges.

Employing the right people to do sensitive and demanding work with vulnerable children is one of the most important factors in operating the 'Authentic Warmth' model of childcare and recruitment requires careful consideration. Psychologist Meredith Kiraly in her 2003 book, *Residential Child Care Staff Selection,* sets out the principles for staff selection and provides a recruitment guide for organisations working with children. Similarly, a report and a 'tool kit' maximising the chances of recruiting high-quality staff (rather than avoiding appointing the 'wrong' people) has been written by Grimwood et al. (2006) and is downloadable from the National Centre for Excellence in Residential Child Care website.

To summarise, the role of the carer is central to achieving positive outcomes for the children in their care and there is no room for mediocrity. Management responsibility is to facilitate and empower residential and foster carers doing their job, and such support will range from ensuring appropriate training on direct work with the child (the *how?*), psychological theory (the *why?*), support in the form of supervision (the *now what?*) and appropriate financial incentives for achieving meaningful attachments with the children.

3 Leadership

On Paul's eleventh birthday his grandparents had bought him a bike, which he wanted to ride to school, Steven had smashed up his bedroom and had barricaded himself in his room with a broken wardrobe. Mrs Davis, a senior member of staff (and Steven's highly successful key worker) had phoned in sick, Lynn's school had phoned to inform us that they were suspending her because she had assaulted her classroom assistant, and they wanted us to collect her as soon as possible! Paul's mother was visiting him and was demanding to know how he bruised his shin and insisting that he should not be allowed to take his bike on the road. Meanwhile, the one local authority, which had three children in the children's home, but had not paid their invoices for three months, had caused a payroll headache ... and then an inspector arrived for an unannounced inspection!

All of the demands listed in the above passage were based on real issues and events that occurred in our children's home: fortunately, not every day is like the one described, but each day does brings different challenges (and possibilities). The scenario does, however, serve to illustrate an important difference between leadership and management, since a competent manager could deal effectively with each of the issues highlighted. This brings us to the third feature for introducing and maintaining the 'Authentic Warmth' model of professional childcare, *the importance of leadership*.

A crucial feature of all good leaders seems to be their ability to look beyond the near horizon, obtain a vision of 'what could be' and then share it with others in a way which inspires them to join in a professional journey towards the vision. On a more mundane level, leadership also demands tenacity to pursue a creative and exciting view of the future, despite the everyday distractions and obstacles.

When pressing day-to-day issues were delegated to the management team in our two children's homes, it became possible to step back and take a strategic view of the organisation. In this case, the director was able to recognise that what had previously been viewed as individual staff shortcomings could be more correctly attributed to organisational factors, like role uncertainty or conflict, a lack of clarity in responsibility, well-meaning but not particularly valued management support, and some low-key organisational demands which greatly reduced carer–child contact time. It was realised that organisational shortcomings (as well as a lack of carer knowledge and skills) needed to be addressed.

The importance of good leadership is a recurring theme in the report, *What works in residential care?* The quote that Clough et al. (2006) selected from the Social Services Inspectorate (SSI) report of 1993 is worth repeating here, as it illustrates the importance and function of good leadership:

[T]he effectiveness of staff in those homes where good practice was observed was based on clear leadership, organised and consistent ways of working, and clarity of purpose. (SSI, 1993, p. 31)

Our examination of the bigger picture (details of which were discussed in Chapter 1) led us to recognise that psychology was the appropriate knowledge base from which to develop a model which would empower care staff not only with clarity of purpose, but also provide insight and develop skills.

Achieving these objectives required strong leadership to overcome understandable, and occasionally inexplicable, resistance and making sure that the new model did not go the way of other well-meaning but short-lasting initiatives. As well as big issues, there were also the more mundane, but essential, financial, logistical and practical problems to respond to, including:

- providing funding for the psychologist consultant
- arranging and delivering management and staff training
- budgeting for the additional costs of staff time to attend the training and consultation sessions
- ensuring that managers understood and supported the new philosophy
- enabling managers to support their teams by ensuring that carers understood and followed up agreed strategies with individual children
- working with individual staff to get them to understand and to evaluate their own 'parenting style'.

Interestingly, this last point on parenting style provided the director of the children's home (and joint author of this book) with significant insights into the issue of leadership. It is no coincidence that the key components of good parenting which make up the three-dimensional, parenting style model (detailed in Chapter 2) also provide a good practice model for leadership of the children's home where the 'Authentic Warmth' approach to professional childcare was first developed, Indeed, one author used the same three-dimensional model to evaluate his leadership style and discovered that while scoring highly on *level of interest and sensitivity to staff*, his scores on setting boundaries and having clear and high expectations were much lower than expected. In summary, the parenting style dimensions, which support long-term positive outcomes for children, transferred easily to the style of leadership employed by the director of our children's homes by highlighting both assets and areas for improvement.

However, the introduction of change requires more than a vision; innovation demands careful planning, a recognition of current organisational and human resources, and contingency strategies accepted for unpredicted obstacles and problems. It also requires recognition of the energy involved to get a new approach system established with its own time-embedded processes. Bringing about change in organisations is fraught with difficulties for the innovator, as Georgiades and Phillimore (1975, p. 315) have reminded us, the fact of the matter is that 'organisations such as schools and hospitals (and children's homes) will, like dragons, eat hero-innovators for lunch'.

Measuring Care Standards

The Scottish Executive (2005) has developed a set of principles to be used as a framework to evaluate the quality of care provided, and all residential care homes and residential schools are required to work to these standards. These national standards (see Appendix 3 for a reader-friendly summary of the main criteria) are particularly unusual in that the rights of the child or young person appear to be at their epicentre. As such, they represent some of the important and desirable components for care staff and managers to use as good practice guidelines and for care commissioners to consider when placing a child in residential care.

Concluding Comments

Getting everything and everyone to work together in an organisation, as Anglin (2002) pointed out, is a 'struggle for congruence' and it is difficult to see how such congruence could be achieved without a clear practice model to which everyone subscribes. When each member of a childcare team (including the consultant psychologist) understands and shares the childcare approach, is clear about their role and the roles of others, and is supported by clear leadership, direction and management, then the sum of their efforts far exceeds that of even the most committed collection of individuals, working independently.

Organisational capacity building (see McKinsey and Co., 2001) is a concept, which many managers have found helpful in identifying the layers of change, which need to occur if an innovatory approach, like the 'Authentic Warmth' model of childcare is to survive and flourish. This concept involves increasing the capacity of the following dimensions within an organisation:

- *The organisation itself*: to enable it to manage and respond to the increasing and constantly changing demands, which arise internally and, in the outside world.
- *The management*: to acquire the skills and knowledge to cope with both the internal and external expectations.
- *The carers and others who have direct contact with the children and young people*: to improve the ability to carry out key tasks, especially responding to the needs of the children in their care.

In retrospect, it required co-ordinated efforts at all these levels to bring about, support and maintain the changes demanded by the introduction of a new approach to professional care. Indeed, the most powerful message emerging from this chapter is not to underestimate the hurdles and difficulties involved in introducing new and radical practice into an existing organisation, but an equally powerful message is that success can bring new confidence and enthusiasm to directors, managers, carers and their supporting professionals, and to children and young people who were more inclined to value time with their carer.

The most obvious short-term changes were observed in the carers who could manage their everyday work more easily using the individual care plans, which incorporated learning and management strategies, knowledge and understanding of the trauma process and creative responses to behaviour which had previously seemed illogical, unprovoked and unreasonable. As a consequence, carers were less inclined to give up on the child and more ready to 'go the extra mile'.

One serendipitous outcome of our work was the increased level of tolerance and understanding from the teams. Staff derived a feeling of empowerment resulting from their (often new) understanding of what the child was going through, having an agreed action plan for each child, which included a focus on strengths, as well as methods and strategies for working through difficulties, and which confirmed the importance of their own roles in the lives of the children.

Time for Reflection

If carers have unresolved personal issues which predispose them to use emotional or physical maltreatment in their attempts to impose discipline on children, or which prevent them from understanding the psychological needs of children who have been rejected, neglected and abused, should managers be considering whether such a punitive style would require the carer to undergo extensive retraining in childcare, or given advice on choosing an alternative career outside childcare?

Note

1   It is recognised that not all carers are benevolent and that some carers may abuse their power by behaving towards children in ways that are unfair, devaluing or vindictive. This important management issue is addressed in a later section, but, as Georgiades and Phillimore (1975) have recommended, it is always more effective for change agents to direct their initial efforts towards the 'healthy parts' of the organisation.

9
Into the Future

The dreams that we dream for our children never come true, nor are they wholly in vain.
(Bruno Bettelheim, 1903–90, psychologist and writer)

This book has described a journey that started with the realisation that for many children and young people in public care, all was not well, and ended in a carefully worked out model of childcare, designed to deliver quality parenting with sensitive support to children and young people who had received emotionally damaging life experiences. This 'Authentic Warmth' model works because its components are derived from psychological research and theory and because these can be delivered by carers who really do care.

We believe that the 'Authentic Warmth' approach to childcare has benefits for children and carers alike and represents a step towards an enlightened and effective professional curriculum for the adults who support children who have been neglected, rejected and abused. However, before looking to the future with optimism and enthusiasm, in this chapter we will also discuss some of the obstacles to delivering 'Authentically Warm' care (or any enlightened system which attempts to aid vulnerable children on their journey to emotional recovery).

Child-unfriendly Trends in our Society

There are potential weaknesses in our 'Authentic Warmth' approach; we make some assumptions that may not square with the reality of life in twenty-first-century Britain, the first being that 'society actually gives a damn'. Even today, in our 'sophisticated' society, we can still witness a scene in which a cynical crowd can shout encouragement to 'Jump!' to a suicidal teenager, while police attempted to talk him down from a ledge.[1]

Less dramatically, but equally worrying are the hardening of attitudes to children in the UK, where an unfriendly and unwelcoming culture towards children seems to be emerging. Many children are now born into an impersonal, hospital-based, medically dominated environment. Just when the newborn needs the comfort and contact of its mother, it is common for much of the first 24 hours of a baby's life to be spent in a transparent hospital cot, despite this being a critical time for both mother and baby to bond. Jackson (1999) describes one way that the isolation process can be made acceptable:

We are encouraged to picture our babies lying in their own rooms at night, surrounded by fluffy bunnies and pastel-coloured alphabets. To deny this image is to destroy the whole vision of motherhood for many women in the west. (p. 75)

In our modern world, the practices of sleeping separately from our babies and allowing them to 'cry themselves to sleep' would be viewed as 'abusive' in many non-western cultures. In her book *Kids*, anthropologist Meredith Small notes that close contact was a feature of child–carer relationships among hunter-gatherers; babies in hunter-gatherer societies sleep with and are carried around by their mother, enjoying the close physical contact of the mother and being soothed by the movement of her body. In such societies, children are also valued for their contributions and they do their share of chores, but they also enjoy the love, support and protection of an extended family. Highlighting the importance of studying hunter-gatherer societies in order to understand human evolution, the author concludes with the thought-provoking point: 'that's how our species spent 99 percent of our history' (Small, 2001, p. 18).

Stepping outside our culture can provide an alternative perspective. Cross the English Channel and even this short journey can highlight subtle, but significant, differences in attitudes to children. In general, people tend to be welcoming to children and their evening meal is a family occasion. Unlike their British counterparts, French teenagers appear to enjoy spending time with the family and are included in all family occasions. The observable enthusiasm and affection for children seems to increase with distance from Britain – most Italian and Spanish adults celebrate the presence of little ones at all social events and most Greek children feel adored and valued.

Conversely, in modern England, we seem to take pride in excluding children – hotels in Britain advertise as a benefit, 'Child-free zone' or 'Exclusively for adults' or most bluntly of all 'No children allowed'. Nowadays, some restaurant owners even invoke 'health and safety' regulations as excuses for not offering bottle warming and baby food heating.

These glimpses of the uncaring culture for children reflect the world for children in 'normal' family life. For children 'in need' the picture is even more grim and, as the BBC documentary[2] *No Pets, No Children* claims, the level and quality of support for homeless families has deteriorated since the making of the classic documentary *Cathy Come Home* in 1966.

Children in care, have the worst of all worlds, since they have had to survive parents who are unable or unwilling to look after them, a society which 'Couldn't

Care Less'[3] and the arm's-length 'care' culture, which even the most caring of carers find compelled to offer in order to avoid accusations of abuse, in the current, paranoid, politically correct, risk-averse, child over-protection culture which has become the norm in our current carer workforce.

Although central government may recognise the therapeutic dimension of physical affection, many carers and teachers now feel anxious or discouraged to even touch a child, and in the 2008 Centre for Social Justice report *Couldn't Care Less* a strong plea to bring touch back into childcare was made, one contributor describing the commonly practised hands-off procedures in professional childcare as a 'form of psychological abuse'.

Yet there is a deep psychological need for human affection. This was movingly revealed in one of the stories that emerged after the assassination of President John F. Kennedy (JFK) when his son, John, turned to of one of JFK's work associates and enquired if he was 'a Daddy'. When the work colleague replied that he was, little John asked 'then, will you throw me up in the air?' It is hoped that the White House aide met this poignant request with compassion rather than circumspection!

In their carefully argued journal article, Piper and Smith (2002) refer to 'touch' as an area where adult fear and confusion have led to a situation where the care needs of children have been ignored and neglected, and similarly the need for clarification was highlighted by a care leaver in the Centre for Social Justice (2008) report as follows:

> I hardly ever got a hug from anyone, I went through a couple of years without a hug. Most children get a hug every day, it is unhealthy not to. Not enough emphasis has gone into this. (p. 120, s. 4.5.5)

While anecdotal accounts are fascinating and provide informal illuminations of what appears to be an ever-increasing, child-unfriendly culture, more formal evidence that this British malady may be endemic, can be found in the UNICEF *Report Card* 7 published in 2007. This report puts the UK at the bottom of the league on five out of six dimensions of child well-being that were assessed for 20 countries in Europe plus the USA (see Table 9.1).

Likewise, in October 2008, the United Nations Committee on the Rights of the Child published a report, which severely criticised the UK government for the continued failure to meet international standards on the treatment of children. While this report details many aspects of policy relating to children in the UK, their observations and recommendations on children who have been neglected and/or abused is of particular relevance:

Table 9.1 A summary table of child poverty in perspective

The chart below presents the findings of *Report Card* in summary form. Countries are listed in order of their average rank for the six dimensions of child well-being that have been assessed.[1] A light background indicates a place in the top third of the table; mid-shade denotes the middle third and dark the bottom third.

Dimensions of child well-being	Average ranking position (for all 6 dimensions)	Dimension 1 Material well-being	Dimension 2 Health and safety	Dimension 3 Educational well-being	Dimension 4 Family and peer relationships	Dimension 5 Behaviours and risks	Dimension 6 Subjective well-being
Netherlands	4.2	10	2	6	3	3	1
Sweden	5.0	1	1	5	15	1	7
Denmark	7.2	4	4	8	9	6	12
Finland	7.5	3	3	4	17	7	11
Spain	8.0	12	6	15	8	5	2
Switzerland	8.3	5	9	14	4	12	6
Norway	8.7	2	8	11	10	13	8
Italy	10.0	14	5	20	1	10	10
Ireland	10.2	19	19	7	7	4	5
Belgium	10.7	7	16	1	5	19	16
Germany	11.2	13	11	10	13	11	9
Canada	11.8	6	13	2	18	17	15
Greece	11.8	15	18	16	11	8	3
Poland	12.3	21	15	3	14	2	19

Table 9.1 (Continued)

Dimensions of child well-being	Average ranking position (for all 6 dimensions)	Dimension 1 Material well-being	Dimension 2 Health and safety	Dimension 3 Educational well-being	Dimension 4 Family and peer relationships	Dimension 5 Behaviours and risks	Dimension 6 Subjective well-being
Czech Republic	12.5	11	10	9	19	9	17
France	13.0	9	7	18	12	14	18
Portugal	13.7	16	14	21	2	15	14
Austria	13.8	8	20	19	16	16	4
Hungary	14.5	20	17	13	6	18	13
United States	18.0	17	21	12	20	20	–
United Kingdom	18.2	18	12	17	21	21	20

[1]OECD countries with insufficient data to be included in the overview: Australia, Iceland, Japan, Luxembourg, Mexico, New Zealand, the Slovak Republic, South Korea, Turkey.

Source: UNICEF (2007, p. 2).

50. The Committee regrets that there is still no comprehensive system of recording and analysing abuses committed against children and that mechanisms of physical and psychological recovery and social reintegration for victims are not sufficiently available across the State party.

51. The Committee recommends that the State party:

a.) establish mechanisms for monitoring the number of cases and the extent of violence, sexual abuse, neglect, maltreatment or exploitation, including within the family, in schools and in institutional or other care; b.) ensure that professionals working with children (including teachers, social workers, medical professionals, members of the police and the judiciary) receive training on their obligation to report and take appropriate action in suspected cases of domestic violence affecting children;

b.) strengthen support for victims of violence, abuse, neglect and maltreatment in order to ensure that they are not victimized once again during legal proceedings;

c.) provide access to adequate services for recovery, counselling and other forms of reintegration in all parts of the country. (OHCHR, 2008, p. 12)

Given that the United Nations report was partly informed by the four UK children's commissioners of England, Wales, Northern Ireland and Scotland, there is much to be concerned about. Working within such a background, even enthusiastic foster parents or residential care workers might be forgiven for thinking 'why do we bother?'. The answer is simple; they still hang on to their belief that making a difference in the life of one child makes all their efforts worthwhile.

This leads to our second uncertain assumption that policy- and decision-makers will respond to data rather than dictum and that, at this point in history, will initiate some fundamental changes in our existing childcare system by:

1 Grasping the significance of the messages from the surveys carried out by bodies like the United Nations, as well as the theory and research in psychology, which have highlighted the need for change and the type of support that is needed to meet the needs of neglected, abused and rejected children.
2 Converting this knowledge into legalisation, which supports good practice in childcare.
3 Achieving cross-party consensus to achieve national consistency in childcare and strategic planning for the future (as opposed to all-too-frequent political short-term vote-catching initiatives).
4 Ensuring that public expenditure decisions for children in need, provide the resources which allow civil servants and local government officers to

discharge their duties effectively and the freedom to make strategic investments to achieve long-term results (as opposed to feeling pressurised to achieve short-term cost-saving solutions and only reacting to problems when these reach a critical stage).

5   Accepting that the long-term cost to society will be considerably less by spending money on prevention or when this fails, providing quality therapeutic parenting and care for traumatised children who have endured abuse, neglect and rejection.

6   Understanding the importance of adopting a longer-term perspective for the upbringing of all children. In 'As long as it takes' which is a report published by the charity, Action for Children has highlighted the lack of consistency in childcare policy since 1987:

> There have been over 400 different initiatives, strategies, funding streams, legislative acts and structural changes to services affecting children and young people over the past 21 years. This is equivalent to over 20 different changes faced by children's services for every year since 1987. (Clay et al., 2008, p. 4)

Evil With and Without Intent

In Chapter 8 we discussed the ever-presence of abusive adults and the need to ensure that not only should mega-efforts be made to keep this dangerous group out of the childcare profession, but that the existence of such people should not be allowed to distort the kindness of the majority of people working with children.

An unintended consequence of the need to safeguard children and young people from these dangerous people has been that, the very children who need to receive an excess of affection (to compensate for parental rejection) find themselves unloved and untouchable because of a childcare workforce which is often demoralised, weary and guarded in its spontaneity. Dealing rationally with this issue requires managers and directors who are able to take a broader perspective of affection by putting the needs of the child as the priority, and not just paying lip-service to the concept. To do this requires strong leadership, insight and sensible guidance from within an organisation; however, this particular issue will also need to be grasped at the highest levels within the profession, politically and legally by people who can feel empowered to do so.

There is currently in the UK, an insidious form of child abuse that would appear to be shrouded in a conspiracy of inaction. Whereas, in the 1970s and 1980s, a child in care who had experienced two or more placement breakdowns would have set off a series of professional alarm bells and prompted an emergency review, today, 20-plus placement breakdowns are not uncommon (see psychologists, Jackson and McParlin, 2006, or the statement by the chair of the Social Care Inspection Service, Dame Denise Platt, 2006) and the professional alarm bells are muted. What is now expected is that some children should be able to move without protest from one set of carers or foster parents to a new set, from one home to another, one bed to a different bed, not once or twice but a staggering 20-plus times. In a society that appears to be so concerned about child abuse, why is this form of abuse so widely accepted?

Psychologist Philip Zimbardo (2007) in his book *The Lucifer Effect* has argued that human systems and policies can both generate and maintain empathic or inhuman behaviour. In the case of the latter, Zimbardo has consistently challenged the 'bad apple' view of people who behave in inhuman ways and argued for a 'bad barrel' explanation, a defence he used to explain the ill-treatment of prisoners in Abu Ghraib, the notorious US forces-run prison in Iraq. In the context of looked-after children in the UK, the fact that multiple placement breakdowns have become an accepted national phenomenon suggests that something is seriously flawed with the system. However, this does not mean that social workers, their team leaders, placement officers, commissioners and directors of children's services can breathe a collective sigh of relief, since flawed systems do not excuse individual responsibility. Indeed, Zimbardo (2007) has argued that: '"Bad systems" create "bad situations" create "bad apples" create "bad behaviours" even in good people' (p. 445).

Yet, it only takes one individual to make a stand, in order to expose and question 'bad systems' and undesirable social influences. Zimbardo advocates 'heroism' and provides a 10-step programme (www.LuciferEffect.com) which is designed to resist bad systems, increase the individuals' 'self-awareness, situational sensitivity and street smarts' (p. 452) and promote personal resilience and civic virtue.

Placement breakdowns are likely to damage and dehumanise children, undermine carers' confidence, question the whole childcare profession's professional integrity and expertise, and are incompatible with a recovery programme (including the 'Authentic Warmth' approach). We recommend that when the reader gets to end of this paragraph, they visit Zimbardo's website and apply his 10-step programme to their own practice. Of course, those in power could change the system – implementing the recommendations of the United Nations Committee on the Rights of the Child would go a long way towards this.

If we are to learn from the mistakes of the past, we need to be conversant with both the achievements and mistakes of the past, just as the late Barbara Kahan was in her report 'Residential casework after Waterhouse: swings and roundabouts in child care policy & practice. Fifty Years 1948–1998.' Her recommendations for central and local government remain as fresh and relevant today as they did in 2000:

Central government should:

1. Carry out the Response to the Utting report [1997]
2. Improve social work and residential care training
3. Provide strong inspection capability
4. Build on new initiative of listening to children and young people
5. Encourage in various ways interdisciplinary training
6. Fund research on paedophiles and related issues.

Local Government should:

1. Redress the seriously flawed approach to residential child care – not just their own – but its use generally, including taking training seriously.
2. Use proper staff selection including multi-faceted selection process, contacting previous employers, rigorous vetting checks.
3. Be more realistic about the capacity of fostering.
4. Develop joint training and activities between residential staff and foster carers.
5. Insist on managerial posts involved in decision making and monitoring residential care having appropriate experience and training.
6. Carry out realistic costings of various methods of care.
7. Insist on proper communication between field and residential social workers.

Professional Groups tasks:

1. Within social work the often-unthinking prejudice against group care needs to be confronted.
2. Social workers need to press for better training facilities – e.g. at least an extra year and more post qualifying training and training in understanding and addressing some specific areas of interpersonal behaviour – e.g. heterosexual sexuality in cohabitation, children's sexuality, knowledge of sexual aberrations.
3. Development of specialist resources for supervision and staff development whilst in post.
4. Development of interdisciplinary activities and understanding between doctors, lawyers, social workers, teachers, nurses, police.
5. Development of greater understanding between social workers and teachers.

Training issues:

1. Many of the previous points imply development of various kinds of training – both full time and within the context of working jobs.
2. Trainers selecting students need to be selecting as rigorously as staff in post should be selected.

3. When these various changes are taking place – it is important to carry the trainers with them. Currently some trainers in social work perpetuate old prejudices against group care – and sometimes lack understanding of the context in which people do their work. (Kahan, 1999, pp. 13–15)

A Brighter Future?

While we have argued that too much of the government's efforts have been directed at the symptoms rather than the causes, we have also acknowledged that the massive public expenditure by the government to improve outcomes for children in public care, is evidence of a political will to do the right thing. So, while it is unlikely that enlightenment will happen in the very near future, there are already glimmers of a brighter future for children in public care.

The Children's Workforce Development Council (2008) have (as noted in Chapter 7), started the process of identifying training needs which go beyond National Vocational Qualification, Level 3. Innovative developments have been emerging from the Scottish Institute for Residential Child Care (SIRCC), which is developing specific training to degree level, from the Mary Walsh Institute which now provides a range of higher education and training programmes designed to 'professionalise' childcare, and from a number of initiatives by the National Centre for Excellence in Residential Child Care. All of these represent a counterbalance to the numerous central government, 'three-year-term-of-office quick-fixes', which have ignored the longer-term view needed for work with children and young people who have complex problems.

We never fail to be touched by the sheer volume of kindness, patience, compassion and goodwill among the carers that we talk to, yet suspect that the following social worker disclosure from the book on *Loss, Bereavement and Grief* must often apply to many:

> I want to mop up their tears and make everything all right again, and you can't. So sometimes, I get enmeshed in their grief as well and feel as helpless and hopeless as they do … And I feel like I'm a little beetle on my back, with my legs in the air, struggling to get the right way up, and so is the client. (Spall and Callis, 1997, p. 41)

The Pillars of Parenting offers a vision of a brighter future for those directly involved in the care of other people's children. Its starting point has been the best and most relevant knowledge available to inform and improve professional parenting and support by qualified childcare professionals who not only know what to do, but why to do it. Its endpoint is a happier and enriching future for children and young people in public care who did not deserve their early life experiences but who do deserve a fulfilling adulthood.

Time for Reflection

As a result of reading this book, what can I do to improve the lives of children and young people in public care? In particular, what realistic objectives will I achieve:

- By the end of this week?
- By the end of three months?
- By the end of this year?

Notes

1   An account of this morally reprehensible event appeared under the heading of 'Suicide teenager urged to jump by baying crowd' in the *Daily Telegraph* (30 September, 2008).
2   This programme was shown on BBC 1 on the 28 November 2006.
3   *Couldn't Care Less* is the title of a report published in September, 2008 by the Centre for Social Justice, which details these issues

Appendix 1
A Sample of Questions Included in the Broaden and Build Checklist for Organisations Wishing to Bring about Fundamental Changes in their Support for Children and Young People Who Are in Public Care

Pillars of Parenting
Living Psychology

This checklist focuses on the psychological needs of the child or young person in residential care and the assumption is that other prerequisites, like care and protection are already in place. The 'Broaden and Build Checklist' is designed to highlight organisational features of the residential home which would support the 'Authentic Warmth' model of professional childcare and is divided into three main areas – family environment, therapeutic care and the restoration of 'normality'.

(a) Creating a family living environment *while removing the emotional intensity and negativity of the original family*

➤ Ensuring a 'good beginning' when the child comes to live in your residential home.
➤ Maintaining high levels of staff optimism and enthusiasm about children and young people in general and individuals in particular.
➤ Helping staff to keep the needs of children and young people at the forefront of their everyday and preventing staff from being distracted by trite/low level demands on their time.
➤ etc.

Notes:

(b) Responding to the trauma-based behaviour of many children and young people in public care

➤ demonstrating to the child that he or she matters to you.
➤ responding appropriately to affection
➤ supporting the efforts of the child or young person to adapt to some of the negative life experiences that they have experienced
➤ etc.

Notes:

(c) Developing a sense of normality, security and belonging

➤ ensuring high levels of carer–child engagement throughout the day
➤ supporting the child or young person in school
➤ enabling the child or young person to achieve the balance between rights and responsibilities.
➤ etc.

Notes:

Key points for discussion with director and senior management

➤

➤

➤

Key source: Anglin (2004).

25-02-08

Appendix 2
A Summary of the 'Authentic Warmth' Model of Professional Childcare

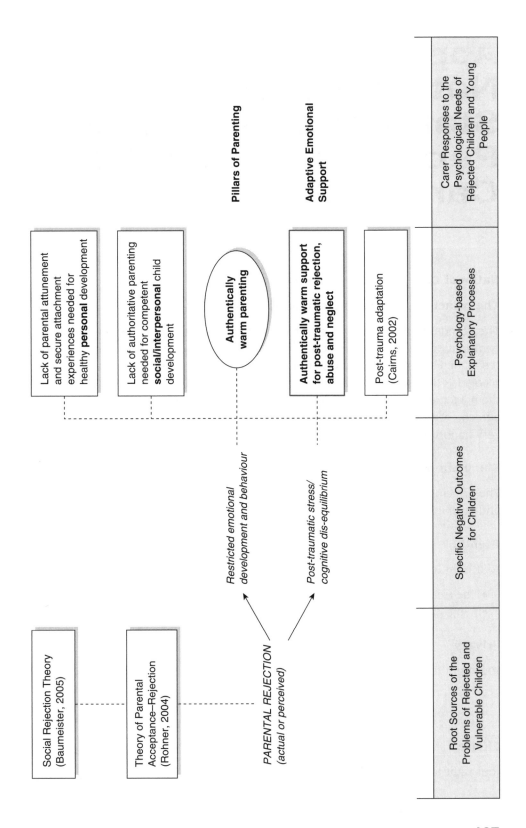

Social Rejection Theory
(Baumeister, 2005)

Theory of Parental
Acceptance–Rejection
(Rohner, 2004)

PARENTAL REJECTION
(actual or perceived)

Restricted emotional
development and behaviour

Post-traumatic stress/
cognitive dis-equilibrium

Lack of parental attunement
and secure attachment
experiences needed for
healthy **personal** development

Lack of authoritative parenting
needed for competent
social/interpersonal child
development

**Authentically
warm parenting**

Pillars of Parenting

**Authentically warm support
for post-traumatic rejection,
abuse and neglect**

Post-trauma adaptation
(Cairns, 2002)

**Adaptive Emotional
Support**

Root Sources of the
Problems of Rejected and
Vulnerable Children

Specific Negative Outcomes
for Children

Psychology-based
Explanatory Processes

Carer Responses to the
Psychological Needs of
Rejected Children and Young
People

Appendix 3
National Care Standards for Young People in Residential Care in Scotland

National Care Standards for Scotland

The principles behind the standards

The standards are based on a set of principles that are the result of all the contributions made by the NCSC, its working groups and everyone else who responded to the consultations on the standards as they were being written. They recognise that services must be accessible and suitable for everyone who needs them, including people from minority ethnic communities. They reflect the strong agreement that you have rights and that your experience of receiving services is very important and should be positive.

The main principles

The principles are dignity, privacy, choice, safety, realising potential and equality and diversity.

Dignity

Your right to:

- be treated with dignity and respect at all times; and
- enjoy a full range of social relationships.

Privacy

Your right to:

- have your privacy and property respected; and
- be free from unnecessary intrusion.

Choice

Your right to:

- make informed choices, while recognising the rights of other people to do the same;
- know about the range of choice; and
- get help to fully understand all the options and choose the one that is right for you.

Safety

Your right to:

- feel safe and secure in all aspects of life, including health and well-being;
- be secure in the knowledge that adults are responsible for children's safety;
- enjoy safety but not be over-protected; and
- be free from exploitation and abuse.

Realising potential

Your right to have the opportunity to:

- achieve all you can;
- make full use of the resources that are available to you; and
- make the most of your life.

Equality and diversity

Your right to:

- live an independent life, rich in purpose, meaning and personal fulfilment;
- be valued for your ethnic background, language, culture and faith;
- be treated equally and be cared for in an environment which aims to be free from bullying harassment and discrimination; and
- be able to complain effectively without fear of victimisation. The Scottish Commission for the Regulation of Care

Reproduced by permission of the Scottish Executive National Care Standards Committee (2005) *National Care Standards: Care homes for children and young people*. Edinburgh: Scottish Executive and Blackwells Bookshop.

References

Chapter 1

Children's Workforce Development Council (2008) *The State of the Children's Social Care Workforce*, www.cwdcouncil.org.uk/assets/0000/2257/CWDC_State_of_the_Social_Care_Workforce_2008_version_3_310708.pdf

Cunningham, H. (2006) *The Invention of Childhood*. London: BBC Books.

Dent, J.R. and Cameron, R.J. (2003) 'Developing resilience in children who are in public care; the educational psychology perspective', *Educational Psychology*, 19(1): 3–19.

Department for Education and Skills (2003) 'Choice protects: facts and figures', www.dfes.gov.uk/choiceprotects/factsandfigures

Department for Education and Skills (2005a) *A Children's Workforce Strategy: A Strategy to Build a World-class Workforce for Children and Young People*. Nottingham: DfES Publications.

Department for Education and Skills (2005b) 'Every Child Matters: change for children in social care', www.everychildmatters.gov.uk/socialcare

Department for Education and Skills (2006) *Care Matters: Transforming the Lives of Children and Young People in Care*. Nottingham: DfES Publications.

Department for Education and Skills (2007) *Care Matters: Time for Change*. Nottingham: DfES Publications.

Department of Health (2000) *The Quality Protects Programme: Transforming Children's Services 2000/01 – District Council's Role (5th June 2000)*. London: HMSO.

Forrester, D., Goodman, K., Cocker, C., Binnie, C. and Jensch, G. (2008) *What Is the Impact of Care on Children's Welfare? A Focussed Review of the Literature prepared for the Welsh Assembly Government*. Cardiff: Welsh Assembly.

Jackson, S. and Martin, P.Y. (1998) 'Surviving the care system: education and resilience', *Journal of Adolescence*, 21: 569–83.

Jackson, S. and McParlin, P. (2006) 'The education of children in care', *The Psychologist*, 19(2): 90–3.

Leckman, J.F. and Bennett, L.L. (2008) Editorial: 'A global perspective of child and adolescent mental health', *Journal of Child Psychology and Psychiatry, Annual Research Review*, 49(3): 221–5.

Office of National Statistics (2005) Information available on the 'Every Child Matters' website, www.everychildmatters.gov.uk/socialcare/lookedafterchildren/factsandfigures/

UNICEF (2007) 'Child poverty in perspective: An overview of child well-being in rich countries', *Innocenti Report Card 7*. Florence: UNICEF Innocenti Research Centre.

Chapter 2

Anglin, J.P. (2004) 'Discovering what makes a "well-enough" functioning residential group setting for children and young people: constructing a theoretical framework and responding to critiques of grounded theory method', in H.G. Erikssohn and T. Tjelflaat (eds), *Residential Care: Horizons for the Next Century*. Aldershot: Ashgate.

Barber, B.K. (1996) 'Psychological control: revisiting a neglected construct', *Child Development*, 67: 3296–319.

Baumeister, R. (2005) 'Rejected and alone', *The Psychologist*, 18(12): 732–5.

Baumrind, D. (1989) 'Rearing competent children', in W. Damon (ed.), *Child Development Today and Tommorrow*. San Francisco, CA: Jossey Bass.

Baumrind, D. (1991) 'The influence of parenting style on adolescent competence and substance use', *Journal of Early Adolescence*, 11: 56–95.

Baumrind, D. (1993) 'The average expectable environment is not good enough', *Child Development*, 64: 1299–317.

Baumrind, D. (2005) 'Patterns of parental authority and adolescent autonomy', in J. Smetana (ed.), *New Directions for Child Development: Changes In Parental Authority During Adolescence*. San Francisco, CA: Jossey-Bass.

Bowlby, J. (1979) *The Making and Breaking of Affectional Bonds*. London: Routledge.

Cameron child, Jessica (1978) 'An autobiography of violence', *Child Abuse and Neglect*, 2: 139–49.

Creighton, S.J. and Tissier, G. (2003) *Child Killings in England and Wales*. London: NSPCC, www.nspcc.org.uk/inform/research/briefings/childkillingsinenglandand wales_wda48218.html

Department for Education and Skills (2005) 'Every Child Matters: Change for Children in Social Care', www.everychildmatters.gov.uk/socialcare

Department of Health (2002) *Children's Homes: National Minimum Standards – Children's Home Regulations*. London: The Stationery Office.

Fonagy, P. (2003) 'Attachment and development of self, and its pathology in personality disorders', *PSYCHOMEDIA*, www.psychomedia.it

Fonagy, P. and Kurtz, Z. (2002) 'Disturbance of conduct', in P. Fonagy, M. Target, D. Cottrell, J. Phillips and Z. Kurtz (eds), *What works for Whom: A Critical Review of Treatments for Children and Adolescents*. New York: Guilford.

Fonagy, P., Steele, M., Steele, H., Higgett, A. and Target, M. (1994) 'The Emanuel Miller Memorial Lecture, 1992: the theory and practice of resilience', *Journal of Child Psychology and Psychiatry*, 35(2): 231–57.

General Social Care Council (2002) *Code of Practice for Social Care Workers and Code of Practice for Employees of Social Care Workers*. London: GSCC.

Gerhardt, S. (2004) *Why Love Matters: How Affection Shapes a Baby's Brain*. Hove: Brunner-Routledge.

Grossman, K.E., Waters, E. and Grossman, K. (2005) *Attachment for Infancy to Adulthood*. New York: Guilford.

Howe, D. (2005) *Child Abuse and Neglect: Attachment, Development and Intervention*. Basingstoke: Palgrave.

Iwaniec, D., Larkin, E. and Sherry, D. (2007) 'Emotionally harmful parenting', *Child Care in Practice*, 13(3): 203–20.

Jackson, S. and Martin, P.Y. (1998) 'Surviving the care system: education and resilience', *Journal of Adolescence*, 21: 569–83.

Jackson, S. and McParlin, P. (2006) 'The education of children in care', *The Psychologist*, 19(2): 90–3.

Leung, K., Lau, S. and Lam, W.-L. (1998) 'Parenting styles and academic achievement: a cross-cultural study', *Merrill-Palmer Quarterly*, 22(2): 157–72.

Newman, T. and Blackburn, S. (2002) *Transition in the Lives of Children and Young People: Resilience Factors*. Edinburgh: Scotland Executive Education Department. Also available from www.scotland.gov.uk/library5/education/ic78-00.asp

Patterson, J., Barlow, J., Mockford, C., Klimes, I., Pyper, C. and Steward-Brown, S. (2002) 'Improving mental health through parenting programmes: block randomised controlled trial', *Archives of Disease in Childhood*, 87: 472–7.

Perry, B.D. (1997) 'Incubated in terror: neuro-developmental factors in the "cycle of violence"', in J.D. Osofstey (ed.), *Children in a Violent Society*. New York: Guilford.

Perry, B.D. (2000) 'Traumatized children: how childhood trauma influences brain development', *The Journal of the California Alliance for the Mentally Ill*, 11(1): 48–51.

Rohner, R.P. (1986) *The Warmth Dimension: Foundations of Parental Acceptance–Rejection Theory*. Beverley Hills, CA: SAGE.

Rohner, R.P. (2004) 'The parental "Acceptance–Rejection Syndrome"', *American Psychologist*, 59(8): 830–40.

Rohner, R.P., Khaleque, A. and Couronoyer, D.E. (2004) 'Parental acceptance–rejection theory, methods and implications', www.cspar.uconn.edu/INTROPAR. HTML

Shore, P. (1997) *Re-thinking the Brain: New Insights into Early Development*. New York: Families and Work Institute.

Svanberg, P.O.G. (1998) 'Attachment, resilience and prevention', *Journal of Mental Health*, 7(6): 543–78.

Worldwide Alternatives to Violence (2005) *The WAVE Report 2005: Violence and What to Do About It*, www.wavetrust.org

Chapter 3

Armon-Jones, C. (1986) *The Social Construction of Emotions*. Oxford: Blackwell.

Avshalom, C., Harrington, H., Milne, B., Amell, J.W., Theodore, R.F. and Moffitt, T.E. (2003) 'Children's behavioural styles at aged three are linked to the adult personality traits at aged 26', *Journal of Personality*, 71: 495–513.

Barna, G. (2007) *Revolutionary Parenting: What the Research Shows Really Works*. Ventura, CA: Barna Group.

Baumeister, R. (2005) 'Rejected and alone', *The Psychologist*, 18(12): 732–5.

Beasley, M.K., Thompson, T. and Davidson, J.A. (2003) 'Resilience in response to life stress: the effects of coping style and cognitive hardiness', *Personality and Individual Differences*, 34(1): 77–95.

Banerjee, R. (2005) 'Getting on with one's peers', *Emotional Literacy Update*, 20: 7–9.

Bostock, L. (2004) *Promoting Resilience in Fostered Children and Young People.* London: Social Care Institute for Excellence.

Bowlby, J. (1953) *Child Care and the Growth of Love.* Baltimore, MD: Pelican Books.

Burnett, P. (1999) 'The relationship between significant others' positive and negative statements, self talk and self esteem', *Child Study Journal*, 29: 39–48.

Cameron, R.J. and Maginn, C. (2008) 'Professional childcare: the Authentic Warmth dimension', *British Journal of Social Work*, 38: 1151–72.

Carpendale, J. and Lewis, C. (2006) *How Children Develop Social Understanding.* Oxford: Blackwell.

Campos, J.J., Mumme, D.L., Kermoian, R. and Campos, R.G. (1994) 'A functionalist perspective on the nature of emotion', in N.A. Fox (ed.), *The Development of Emotion Regulation: Biological and Behavioral Considerations.* Monographs of the Society for Research in Child Development, 59(2–3, Serial No. 240): 284–303.

Carvallo, M. and Pelham, B.W. (2006) 'When fiends become friends: the need to belong and perceptions of personal and group discrimination', *Journal of Personality and Social Psychology*, 90(1): 94–108.

Cast, A.D. and Burke, P.J. (2002) 'A theory of self-esteem', *Social Forces*, 80: 1041–68.

Children's Workforce Development Council (2007) *Common Assessment Framework for Children and Young People: Managers' Guide.* Leeds: CWDC.

Coleman, J. and Hagell, A. (2007) *Adolescence, Risk and Resilience: Against the Odds.* Chichester: Wiley.

Daniel, B. and Wassell, S. (2002) *Assessing and Promoting Resilience in Vulnerable Children I (Early Years).* London: Jessica Kingsley.

Daniel, B. and Wassell, S. (2005) *Resilience: A Framework for Positive Practice.* Scottish Executive Social Research, Education Department, www.scotland.gov.uk/Resource/Doc/920/0011997.pdf

Dent, R.J. and Cameron R.J. (2003) 'Developing resilience in children who are in public care: the educational psychology perspective', *Educational Psychology in Practice*, 19(1): 3–20.

Department for Education and Skills (2003) 'Choice protects: facts and figures', www.dfes.gov.uk/choiceprotects/factsandfigures

Department for Education and Skills/Department of Health (2000) *Guidance on the education of children and young people in public care.* London: DfES/DOH. (Section 4.3).

Department of Health (2002) *Children's Homes: National Minimum Standards – Children's Homes Regulations.* London: The Stationery Office.

Gardner, W.L., Pickett, C.L. and Brewer, M.B. (2000) 'Social exclusion and selective memory: How the "need to belong" influences memory for social events', *Personality and Social Psychology Bullentin*, 26: 486–96.

Gerhardt, S. (2004) *Why Love Matters: How Affection Shapes a Baby's Brain*. Hove: Brunner-Routledge.

Hagerty, B.M. and Williams, A.R. (1999) 'The effects of sense of belonging, social support, conflict, and loneliness on depression', *Nursing Research*, 48(4): 215–19.

Harré, R. and Gillett, G. (1994) *The Discursive Mind*. London: SAGE.

Havighurst, S.S., Harley, A. and Prior, M. (2004) 'Building preschool children's emotional competence: a parenting program', *Early Education and Development*, 15(4): 423–48.

Health Education Authority (1997) *Mental Health Promotion: A Quality Framework*. London: HEA.

Howe, D. (2005) *Child Abuse and Neglect. Attachment, Development and Intervention*. Basingstoke: Palgrave Macmillan.

Jackson, S. (2002) 'Promoting stability and continuity in care away from home', in D. McNeish, T. Newman and H. Roberts (eds), *What works for children? Effective Services for Children and Families*. Buckingham: Open University Press.

Jackson, S. and Martin, P.Y. (1998) 'Surviving the care system: education and resilience', *Journal of Adolescence*, 21: 569–83.

Jackson, S. and McParlin, P. (2006) 'The education of children in care', *The Psychologist*, 19(2): 90–3.

Katz, L.F. and Gottman, J.M. (1993) 'Patterns of marital conflict predict children's internalizing and externalizing behaviors', *Developmental Psychology*, 29: 940–50.

Kochanska, G. (1991) 'Socialisation and temperament in the development of guilt and conscience', *Child Development*, 62: 1379–92.

Kohn, A. (2005) *Unconditional Parenting: Moving from Rewards and Punishments to Love and Reason*. New York: Atria Books.

Kroger, J. (2004) *Identity in Adolescence: The Balance between Self and Other*. London: Psychology Press.

Lazarus, R.S. (1991) *Emotion and Adaptation*. London: Oxford University Press.

Lewis, R. and Frydenberg, E. (2002) 'Concomitants of failure to cope: what should we teach adolescents about coping?', *British Journal of Educational Psychology*, 27: 419–31.

Lewis, M. and Michalson, L. (1983) *Children's Emotions and Moods: Developmental Theory and Measurement*. New York: Plenum.

Maccoby, E.E. (1999) 'The uniqueness of the parent–child relationship', in W.A. Collins and B. Laursen (eds), *Minnesota Symposium on Child Psychology (No. 29)*. London: Lawrence Erlbaum.

Maslow, A.H. (1971) *The Farther Reaches of Human Nature*. New York: Penguin Compass.

Masten, A.S. and Coatsworth, J.D. (1998) 'The development of confidence in favourable and unfavourable environments: lessons from research on successful children', *American Psychologist*, 53(2): 205–20.

Newman, T. and Blackburn, S. (2002) *Interchange 78. Transitions in the Lives of Children and Young People: Resilience Factors*. Edinburgh: Scottish Executive Education Department.

Piper, H. and Smith, H. (2003) 'Touch in education and child care settings: dilemmas and responses', *British Education Research Journal*, 29(6): 879–94.

Power, F.C., Higgins, A. and Kohlberg, L. (1989) *Lawrence Kohlberg's Approach to Moral Education*. New York: Columbia University Press.

Prior, V. and Glaser, D. (2006) *Understanding Attachment and Attachment Disorders: Theory, Evidence and Practice*. Philadelphia, PA: Jessica Kingsley.

Putnam, R. (1995) 'Bowling alone: America's declining social capital', *Journal of Democracy*, 6(1): 65–78.

Putnam, R. (2000) *Bowling Alone: The Collapse and Revival of the American Community*. New York: Simon & Schuster.

Redler, P. and Lucy, C. (eds) (1995) *Assessment of Parenting: Psychiatric and Psychological Considerations*. London: Routledge.

Reid, R. (1996) 'Research in self-monitoring with students with learning difficulties: the present, the prospects and the pitfalls', *Journal of Learning Disabilities*, 29(3): 317–31.

Rohner, R.P., (2004) 'The parental "acceptance–rejection" syndrome: universal correlates of perceived rejection', *American Psychologist*, 59(8): 827–40.

Rohner, R.P., Khaleque, A. and Couronoyer, D.E. (2005) 'Parental acceptance–rejection theory, methods and implications', http://vm.uconn.earbl.html

Saarni, C. (1999) *The Development of Emotional Competence*. New York: Guilford.

Schofield, G. and Beek, M. (2005) 'Risk and resilience in long-term foster-care', *British Journal of Social Work*, 35(8): 1283–300.

Sedikides, C. (2005) 'Close relationships: what's in it for us?', *The Psychologist*, 18(8): 490–3.

Steinberg, L. (2004) *Ten Basic Principles of Good Parenting*. New York: Simon & Schuster.

Svanberg, P.O.G. (1998) 'Attachment, resilience and prevention', *Journal of Mental Health*, 7(6): 543–78.

Tajfel, H. and Turner, J.C. (1986) 'The social identity theory of inter-group behavior', in S. Vworchel and L.W. Austin (eds), *Psychology of Inter-group Relations*. Chicago, IL: Nelson–Hall.

Worldwide Alternatives to Violence (WAVE) (2005) *The WAVE Report 2005: Violence and What to Do About It*, www.wavetrust.org

Zimmerman, B.J. (1994) 'Dimensions of academic self-regulation: a conceptual framework for education', in D.H. Schunk and B.J. Zimmerman (eds), *Self-regulation of Learning and Performance: Issues and Educational Applications*. Hillsdale, NJ: Lawrence Erlbaum.

Chapter 4

Audit Commission (1996) *Misspent Youth: Young People and Crime.* London: HMSO.

Bailey, S. (2002) Keynote presentation to the Conference on Children Lost – Serious and violent crime: intervention and prevention, organised by the Bridge Child Care Development Consultancy at SOAS, 5 July.

Baumrind, D. (1967) 'Child care practices anteceding three patterns of pre-school behaviour', *Genetic Psychology Monographs*, 75: 43–8.

Baumrind, D. (1991) 'The influence of parenting style on adolescent competence and substance use', *Journal of Early Adolescence*, 11: 56–95.

Cambridgeshire County Council (2003) *Behaviour Management in Cambridgeshire Social Services Residential Children's Homes.* Cambridge: Cambridgeshire County Council Social Services.

Cameron, R.J. (1998) 'School discipline in the United Kingdom: promoting classroom behaviour, which encourage effective teaching and learning', *School Psychology Review*, 27(1): 33–44.

Caspi, A., Moffitt, T.E., Newman, D.L. and Silva, P.A. (1996) 'Behavioural observations at age 3 years predict adult psychiatric disorders', *Archives of General Psychiatry*, 53: 1033–9.

Davidson, J.C., McCullough, D., Steckley, L. and Warren, T. (eds) (2005) *Holding Safely: Guidance for Residential Child Care Practitioners and Managers about Physically Restraining Children and Young People.* Glasgow: Scottish Institute for Residential Child Care.

Department for Children, Schools and Families (DCSF) (2008) *The Children's Plan: Building Brighter Futures.* Norwich: The Stationery Office.

Department for Education and Skills (DfES) (2001) *Special Educational Needs Code of Practice.* Nottingham: DfES Publications.

Department for Education and Skills (DfES) (2003) *Guidance on the Use of Restrictive Physical Interventions for Pupils with Severe Behavioural Difficulties.* Nottingham: DfES Publications.

Department for Education and Skills (DfES) (2006) *Statutory Guidance on Section 6 Education and Inspections Act (Positive Activities for Young People).* London: DfES Publications.

Department of Health (2002) *Children's Homes: National Minimum Standards – Children's Home Regulations.* London: The Stationery Office.

Dreikurs, R. and Soldz, V. (1964) *Children: The Challenge.* New York: Hawthorn Books.

Dreikurs, R., Grimwald, B.B. and Pepper, F.C. (1982) *Maintaining Sanity in the Classroom: Classroom Management Techniques.* New York: Harper and Row.

Edwards, C.H. and Watts, V. (2004) *Classroom Discipline and Management: An Australian Perspective.* Milton, Queensland: Wiley (Australia Ltd).

Frost, J. (2005) *Supernanny: How to Get the Best from your Children.* London: Hodder & Stoughton.

Gardner, F.E. (1992) 'Parent–child interaction and conduct disorder', *Educational Psychology Review*, 4(6): 135–62.

Geen, R.G. (1990) *Human Aggression*. Pacific Grove, CA: Brookes/Cole.

Gershoff, E.T. (2002) 'Corporal punishment by parents and associated child behaviour and experiences: a meta-analytic and theoretical review', *Psychological Bulletin*, 128(4): 539–79.

HM Treasury/Department for Education and Skills (DfES) (2005) *Support for Parents: The Best Start for Children*. www.hm-treasury.gov.uk

Hoghughi, M. and Long, N. (2004) *Handbook of Parenting: Theory and Research for Practice*. London: SAGE.

Hopkins, B. (2008) 'Restorative approaches in residential childcare', *Highlight No. 242*. London: National Children's Bureau.

Kotchick, B., Shaffer, A., Miller, K. and Forehand, R. (2004) 'Parenting and anti-social children and adolescents', in M. Hoghughi and N. Long (eds) *Handbook of Parenting: Theory and Research for Practice*. London: SAGE.

Lambourn, S.D., Mounts, N.S., Steinberg, L. and Dornbusch, S.M. (1991) 'Patterns of competence and adjustment among adolescents from authoritative, authoritarian, indulgent and neglectful families', *Child Development*, 62: 1049–65.

Leung, K., Lau, S. and Lam, W-L. (1998) 'Parenting styles and academic achievement: a cross-cultural study', *Merrill-Palmer Quarterly*, 22(2): 157–72.

Mainey, A. and Crimmens, D. (2006) *Fit for the Future? Residential Care in the United Kingdom*. London: National Children's Bureau.

McLoyd, B.C. (1990) 'The impact of economic hardship on black families and children: psychological distress, parenting and socio-economic development', *Child Development*, 61: 311–46.

Mental Health Foundation (1999) *Bright Futures*. London: MHF.

Minnis, H. and Del Priori, C. (2001) 'Mental health services for looked-after children: implications from two studies', *Adoption and Fostering Journal*, 25(4): 27–38.

Moyer, K.E. (1976) *The Psychology of Aggression*. New York: Harper and Row.

Nicolas, B., Roberts, S. and Wurr, C. (2003) 'Looked after children in residential homes', *Child and Adolescent Mental Health*, 8(2): 78–83.

O'Neill, R.E., Horner, R.H., Albin, R., Storey, K. and Sprague, J. (1990) *Functional Assessment of Problem Behaviour: A Practical Assessment Guide*. Pacific Grove, CA: Brookes/Cole.

Office for Standards in Education (Ofsted) (2005) *Managing Challenging Behaviour*. London: Ofsted.

Pinker, S. (2002) *The Blank Slate*. London: Penguin/Allen Lane.

Rae, T. and Daly, S. (2008) *Controlling Anger: A Solution Focused Approach for Young People*. London: Optimus.

Rock, R. and Graham, V.S. (2008) *Mama Rock's Rules: 10 Lessons for Raising a Household of Successful Children*. New York: Collins.

Rohner, R.P., Khaleque, A. and Couronover, D.E. (2004) 'Parental acceptance–rejection theory, methods and implications', www.cspar.uconn.edu/INTROPAR.HTML

Sanders, M.R., Turner, K.M. and Markie-Dadds, C. (2002) 'The development and dissemination of the Triple P-Positive Parenting Program: a multilevel, evidence-based system of parenting and family support', *Prevention Science,* 3(3): 173–89.

Scottish Executive Justice Department (2003) *Your Children Matter: Know your Responsibilities and Rights.* Edinburgh: Scottish Executive Justice Department.

Thompson, M.J.J., Stevenson, J., Sonuga-Barke, E., Nott, P., Bhatti, Z., Price, A. and Hudswell, M. (1996) 'Mental health of preschool children and their mothers in a mixed urban/rural population I: prevalence and etiological factors', *British Journal of Psychiatry,* 168: 16–20.

Westmacott, E.V.S. and Cameron, R.J. (1981) *Behaviour Can Change.* Basingstoke: Macmillan.

Willmott, N. (2007) *A Review of the Use of Restorative Justice in Children's Residential Care.* London: National Children's Bureau.

Wilson, D., Sharp, C. and Patterson, A. (2006) *Young Persons and Crime: Findings from the 2005 Offending, Crime and Justice Survey.* London: Home Office Research, Development and Statistics Directorate.

Yoshikawa, H. (1994) 'Prevention as cumulative protection: effects of early family support on chronic delinquency and its risks', *Psychological Bulletin,* 115: 28–54.

Youth Justice Board (2004) *Key Elements of Effective Practice: Restorative Justice.* London: Youth Justice Board.

Chapter 5

Baumeister, R. (2005) 'Rejected and alone', *The Psychologist,* 18(12): 732–5.

Bonanno, G.A. (2004) 'Loss, trauma and human resilience: have we underestimated the human capacity to thrive after extremely aversive events?', *American Psychologist,* 59(1): 20–8.

Bonanno, G.A. and Mancini, A.D. (2008) 'The human capacity to thrive in the face of extreme adversity', *Pediatrics,* 121: 369–75.

Bowlby, J. (1961) 'Children's mourning and its implications for psychiatry', *American Journal of Psychiatry,* 118: 481–98.

Cairns, K. (2002) *Attachment, Trauma and Resilience.* London: British Association for Adoption and Fostering.

Department for Children, Schools and Families (2008) *Outcome Indicators for Children Looked After, Twelve Months to 30 September 2007 – England.* London: Office of National Statistics.

Department for Education and Skills (2007) *Care Matters: Time for Change.* Nottingham: DfES Publications.

Eisenberger, N.I. (2006) 'Identifying the neural correlates underlying social pain: implications for developmental processes', *Human Development*, 49: 273–93.

Eisenberger, N.I., Lieberman, M.D. and Williams, K.D. (2003) 'Does rejection hurt? An fMRI study of social exclusion', *Science,* 303(10): 290–2.

Eisenstadt, J.M. (1978) 'Parental loss and genius', *American Psychologist*, 33: 211–23.

Gilbert, A. (2008) *Deliver Me from Evil: A Sadistic Mother, a Childhood Torn Apart.* London: Pan.

Jackson, S. and Martin, P.Y. (1998) 'Surviving the care system: education and resilience', *Journal of Adolescence*, 21: 569–83.

Joseph, S. and Linley, P.A. (2008) *Trauma, Recovery and Growth: Positive Psychological Perspective of Post-Traumatic Stress.* Chichester: Wiley.

Kubler-Ross, E. and Kessler, D. (2007) *On Grief and Grieving: Finding the Meaning of Life through the Five Stages of Loss.* New York: Scribner Book Company/Simon & Schuster.

Landon, M. (2008) *Daddy's Little Earner*. Glasgow: HarperCollins.

Linley, P.A. (2000) 'Transforming psychology: the example of trauma', *The Psychologist*, 13(7): 353–5.

Linley, P.A. and Joseph, S. (2002) 'Post-traumatic growth', *Counselling and Psychotherapy Journal*, 13(1): 14–17.

Middleton, W., Burnett, P., Raphael, B. and Martinek, N. (1996) 'The bereavement response: a cluster analysis', *British Journal of Psychiatry*, 169: 167–71.

Panksepp, J. (2003) 'Feeling the pain of social loss', *Science*, 303(10): 237–9.

Pelzer, D. (1995) *A Child called 'IT'*. London: BCA.

Perry, B.D. (2000) 'Traumatized children: how childhood trauma influences brain development', *The Journal of the California Alliance for the Mentally Ill,* 11(1): 48–51.

Spry, C. (2008) *Child C: Surviving a Foster Mother's Reign of Terror.* London: Pocket/Simon & Schuster.

Starcevic, V. (2005) 'Fear of death in hypochondriasis: bodily threat and its treatment implications', *Journal of Contemporary Psychotherapy*, 35(3): 227–37.

Tedeschi, R.G. (1999) 'Violence transformed: posttraumatic growth in survivors and their societies', *Aggression and Violent Behavior*, 4(3): 319–41.

Tedeschi, R.G. and Calhoun, L.G. (1995) *Trauma and transformation: Growing in the aftermath of suffering.* Thousand Oaks, CA: SAGE.

Tedeschi, R.G. and Calhoun, L.G. (2004) 'Posttraumatic growth: conceptual foundations and empirical evidence', *Psychological Inquiry*, 15(1): 1–18.

Waldinger, R.J., Schulz, M.S., Barsky, A.J. and Ahern, D.K. (2006) 'Mapping the road from childhood trauma to adult somatization: the role of attachment', *Psychosomatic Medicine*, 68: 129–35.

Chapter 6

Banks, M. and Woolfson, L. (2008) 'Why do students think they fail? The relationship between attributions and academic self-perceptions', *British Journal of Special Education*, 35(1): 49–56.

Burton, S. (2008) 'Empowering learning support assistants to enhance the emotional wellbeing of children in school', *Educational and Child Psychology*, 25(1): 41–56.

Cameron, R.J. (1998) 'School discipline in the United Kingdom: promoting classroom behaviour which encourages effective teaching and learning', *School Psychology Review*, 27(1): 33–44.

Dent, R.J. and Cameron, R.J. (2003) 'Developing resilience in children who are in public care: the educational psychology perspective', *Educational Psychology in Practice*, 19(1): 13–27.

Department for Children, Schools and Families (2008a) *Outcome Indicators for Children Looked After, 12 months to 30th September 2007. England.* London: DCSF.

Department for Children, Schools and Families (2008b) *Permanent and Fixed Period Exclusions form Schools in England 2006/07.* London: DCSF.

Department for Education and Skills (2006) *Care Matters: Transforming the Lives of Children and Young People in Care.* London: The Stationery Office.

Department for Education and Skills (2007) *Care Matters: Time for Change.* Nottingham: Department for Education and Skills.

Dreikurs, R., Grunwald, B.B. and Pepper, F.C. (1982) *Maintaining Sanity in the Classroom: Classroom Management Techniques.* New York: Harper and Row.

Duckworth, A.L. and Seligman, M.E.P. (2005) 'Self-discipline outdoes IQ in predicting academic performance of adolescence', *Psychological Science*, 16: 939–44.

Gallagher, B., Brannan, C., Jones, R. and Westwood, S. (2004) 'Good practice in the education of children in residential care', *British Journal of Social Work*, 34: 1133–60.

Goodenow, C. (1993) 'The psychological sense of school membership among adolescents: scale development and educational correlates', *Psychology in Schools*, 30: 79–90.

Greig, A., Minnis, H., Millward, R., Sinclair, C., Kennedy, E., Towlson, K., Reid, W. and Hill, J. (2008) 'Relationships and learning: a review and investigation of narrative coherence in looked-after children in primary school', *Educational Psychology in Practice*, 24(1): 13–27.

Harker, R.M., Dobel-Obert, D., Lawrence, J., Berridge, D. and Sinclair, R. (2003) 'Who takes care of education? Looked after children's perceptions of support for educational progress', *Child and Family Social Work*, 8(2): 89–100.

Hart, S.W., Brassard, M.R. and Carlson, H.S. (1996) 'Psychological maltreatment', in J. Briere, L. Bostiner, J. Bolkley, C.A. Jenny and T.A. Reid (eds), *The APSAC Handbook on Child Maltreatment.* Thousand Oaks, CA: SAGE.

Health Education Authority (HEA) (1997) *Mental Health Promotion: A Quality Framework.* London: HEA.

Hook, P. and Vass, A. (2004) 'The principle-centred classroom: positive discipline and supportive schools', in E. Haworth (ed.), *Supporting Staff Working with Pupils with Social Emotional and Behavioural Difficulties.* Lichfield: QEd.

Howe, D. (2005) *Child Abuse and Neglect: Attachment, Development and Intervention.* Basingstoke: Palgrave.

Jackson, S. and McParlin, P. (2006) 'The education of children in care', *The Psychologist,* 19(2): 90–3.

Jackson, S. and Martin, P.Y. (1998) 'Surviving the care system: education and resilience', *Journal of Adolescence,* 21: 569–83.

Kendrick, A. (1998) *Education and Residential Care: A Brief Review.* Strathelyde: University of Strathclyde, Scottish Institute for Residential Childcare.

McGrath, H. and Noble, T. (2003) *Bounce Back: A Classroom Resiliency Programme.* South Melbourne: Pearson Education.

McLaughlin, C. (2007) 'Researching the experience of children and young people at school', interdisciplinary conference on 'Well-being in Childhood', Cambridge Institute of Education, 2 July.

McNeely, C.A., Monnemaker, J.M. and Blum R.W. (2002) 'Promoting school connectedness: evidence from the National Longitudinal Study of Adolescent Health', *Journal of School Health,* 72(4): 138–46.

Mental Health Foundation (1999) *Bright Futures: Promoting Children and Young People's Mental Health.* London: Mental Health Foundation.

Miller, A. (2003) *Teachers, Parents and Classroom Behaviour: A Psychosocial Approach.* Maidenhead: Open University Press/McGraw-Hill Education.

Office for Standards in Education (Ofsted) (2005) *Managing Challenging Behaviour.* London: Ofsted.

Ramey, C.T. and Ramey, S.L. (1998) *Right from Birth: Building a Child's Foundation for Life – Birth to 18 Months.* New York: Goddard Press.

Ryan, M. (2006) *Understanding Why.* London: National Children's Bureau.

Seligman, M.E.P. (2002) *Authentic Happiness: Using the New Positive Psychology to Realise your Potential for Deep Fulfilment.* London: Nicholas Brealey.

Sergeant, H. (2006) *Handle with Care: An Investigation into the Care System.* London: Centre for Young Policy Studies.

Chapter 7

Anglin, J.P. (2004) 'Discovering who makes a "well enough" functioning residential group care setting for children and youth: constructing a theoretical framework and responding to critiques of grounded theory method', in H.C. Erikssohn and T. Tjelflaat (eds), *Residential Care: Horizons for the New Century.* Aldershot: Ashgate.

Bar-On, R. and Parker, J.D.A. (2000) *The BarOn Emotional Quotient Inventory: Youth Version (EQ-i: YV): Technical Manual.* Toronto: Multi-Health Systems.

Briere, J. (1996) *Trauma Symptom Checklist for Children (TSCC) – Professional Manual. Lutz,* FL: PAR.

Children's Workforce Development Council (2008) *The State of the Children's Social Care Workforce 2008: Summary Report.* Leeds: CWDC.

Cooperrider, B.L. and Whitney (2000) 'A positive revolution in change', in R. Golembiewski (ed.), *Handbook for Organisational Behaviour*. 2nd edn. New York: Marcel Decker.

Dent, H.R. and Golding, K.S. (2006) 'Engaging the network: consultation for looked-after children', in K.S. Golding, H.R. Dent, R. Nissim and L. Stott (eds), *Thinking Psychologically about Children Who Are Looked-after and Adopted*. Chichester: Wiley.

Dodge, K.A., McClaskey, C.L. and Feldman, E. (1985) 'Situational approach to the assessment of social competences in children', *Journal of Consulting and Clinical Psychology*, 53: 344–53.

Elliot, C.D., Smith, P. and McCulloch, K. (1997) *British Ability Scales – Second Edition – Technical Manual*. Windsor: NFER-Nelson.

EuroPsychT (2001) *A Framework for Education and Training for Psychologists in Europe*. European Community. Leonardo da Vinci Programme.

Evert, J. (2007) *The Authentic Warmth approach to residential childcare: Improving children's social, behavioural, academic and emotional skills*. Diplomarbeit im Fach Psychologie: Universität Bremen.

Fraser, S. and Greenhalgh, T. (2001) 'Coping with complexity: educating for capability', *British Medical Journal*, 323: 799–803.

Frederickson, N. (2002) 'Evidence based practice and educational psychology', *Educational and Child Psychology*, 19(3): 96–111.

Frederickson, N. and Simmonds, E. (in press) 'Assessing social and effective outcomes of inclusion', *British Journal of Special Education*.

Gioia, G.A., Isquith, P.K., Guy, S.C. and Kenworthy, L. (1996) *BRIEF Behaviour Inventory of Executive Function – Professional Manual*. Lutz, FL: PAR.

Graden, J.L. (2004) 'Arguments for change to consultation, prevention and intervention: will school psychology ever achieve this promise?', *Journal of Educational and Psychological Consultation*, 15(3 and 4): 345–59.

HM Inspectorate (education) (2006) *A Framework for Evaluating the Quality of Services and Organisations*. Edinburgh: The Stationery Office Bookshop.

Kennedy, E.K., Cameron, R.J. and Monsen, J. (in press) 'Professional training for effective consultation in educational and child psychology practice: the untapped potential of the reflective scientist-practitioner model', *School Psychology International*.

Kiresuk, T.J., Smith, A. and Cardillo, J.E. (eds) (1994) *Goal Attainment Scaling: Applications, Theory and Measurement*. Hillsdale, NJ: Erlbaum.

Knotek, S.E., Rosenfield, S.A., Gravois, T.A. and Babinski, L.M. (2003) 'The process offering consultee development during instructional consultation', *Journal of Educational and Psychologist Consultation*, 14(3 and 4): 303–28.

Lewis, A.B., Spencer, J.H., Haas, G.L. and Di Vittis, A. (1987) 'Goal attainment scaling: relevance and replicability in follow-up of in-patients', *Journal of Nervous and Mental Disease*, 175 (7): 408–18.

Maines, B. and Robinson, G. (1988) *B/G-STEEM – a Self-Esteem Scale with Locus of Control Items*. Bristol: Lucky Duck.

Mainey, A. and Crimmens, D. (2006) *Fit for the Future? Residential Care in the United Kingdom.* London: National Children's Bureau.

Miller, W.D. and Rollnick, S. (2002) *Motivational Interviewing: Preparing People for Change.* New York: Guilford Press.

Milligan, I. and Stevens, I. (2006) *Residential Childcare: Collaborative Practice.* London: SAGE.

Moore, J. (2005) 'Recognising and questioning the epistemological basis of educational psychology', *Educational Psychology in Practice*, 21(2):103–16.

Morton, J. and Frith, U. (1995) 'Causal modelling: a structural approach to developmental psychopathology', in D. Cichette and D.J. Cohen (eds), *Manual of Developmental Psychopathology.* 1. New York: Wiley, pp. 257–390.

Naglieri, J.A., LeBuffe, P.A. and Pfeiffer, S.I. (1993) *Devereux Behavior Rating Scale – School Form Manual.* San Antonio, TX: The Psychological Corporation and Harcourt Brace.

Parry, G. (1990) *Coping with Crises.* London: BPS Books and Routledge.

Reddy, L.A., Barboza-Whitehead, S., Files, T. and Rubel, E. (2000) 'Clinical focus of consultation outcome research with children and adolescents', *Special Services in Schools,* 16: 1–22.

Ryff, C.D. and Essex, M.J. (1992) 'The interpretation of life experience and well-being: the sample case of relocation', *Psychology and Aging*, 7: 507–17.

Schön, D. (1987) *Educating the Reflective Practitioner.* New York: Jossey-Bass.

Search Institute (2007) 615 First Avenue, N.E., Suite 125, Minneapolis, MN 55413. (www.si@search-institute.org)

Sheridan, S.M., Eagle, J.W., Cowan, R.J. and Mickelson, W. (2001) 'The effects of conjoint behavioural consultation: results of a four-year investigation', *Journal of School Psychology*, 39(45): 361–85.

Sheridan, S.M., Welch, M. and Orme, S.F. (1996) 'Is consultation effective? A review of outcome research', *Remedial and Special Education*, 17(6): 341–54.

Wagner, P. (2000) 'Consultation: developing a comprehensive approach to service delivery', *Educational Psychology in Practice*, 16(1): 9–18.

Chapter 8

Anglin, J.P. (2002) *Pain, Normality and the Struggle for Congruence.* New York: Haworth Press.

Baumrind, D. (1991) 'The influence of parenting style on adolescent competence and substance use', *Journal of Early Adolescence*, 11: 56–95.

Children's Workforce Development Council (CWDC) (2008) *The State of the Children's Social Care Workforce,* www.cwdcouncil.org.uk/assets/0000/2257/CWDC_State_of_the_Social_Care_Workforce_2008_version_3_310708.pdf

Clough, R., Bullock, R. and Ward, A. (2006) *What Works in Residential Child Care? A Review of Research Evidence and the Practical Considerations.* London: National Children's Bureau.

Department for Education and Skills (2003) *Every Child Matters*. Norwich: The Stationery Office.

Georgiades, N.J. and Phillimore, L. (1975) 'The myth of the hero-innovator and alternative strategies for organizational change', in C. Kiernan and P. Woodford (eds), *Behaviour Modification with the Severely Retarded*. Amsterdam: Associated Science Press.

Grimwood, R., Hawkins, K., Gaffney, A. and Biggs, D. (2006) *Selecting the Best Staff: A Toolkit to Help Improve Recruitment of Staff to Work with Children in Residential Settings*. London: National Centre for Excellence in Residential Childcare.

Hicks, L., Gibbs, I., Weatherly, H. and Byford, S. (2007) *Managing Children's Homes – Developing Effective Leadership in Small Organisations*. London: Jessica Kingsley.

Jackson, D. (1999) '*Three in a Bed: The Benefits of Sleeping with Your Baby*. London: Bloomsbury.

Kahan, B. (1999) 'Residential care after Waterhouse: Roundabouts in Child Care Policy & Practice. Fifty Years 1948–1998', report presented by Barbara Kahan OBE at the Inaugural Conference of the Association of Child Abuse Lawyers, Cambridge, 19 March, www.abny.demon.co.uk/acal/RESIDENTIALCHILDCareBKahan.htm (accessed September 2008).

Kiraly, M. (2003) *Residential Child Care Staff Selection: Choose with Care*. New York: Haworth Press.

Mainey, A. and Crimmens, D. (2006) *Fit for the Future? Residential Childcare in the United Kingdom*. London: National Children's Bureau.

McKinsey and Co. (2001) *Effective Capacity Building in Non-profit Organisations*. Washington, DC: Venture Philanthropy Partners.

Scottish Executive (2005) *National Care Standards: Care Homes for Children and Young People*. Edinburgh: Scottish Executive.

Smith, M. (2005) 'Working in the "Life space"', *In Residence*, 2(August), University of Strathclyde; Scottish Institute for Residential Child Care.

Social Services Inspectorate (SSI) (1993) *Corporate Parents. Inspection of Residential Child Care Services in 11 Local Authorities, November 1992–March 1993*. London: Department of Health.

Winnicott, D.W. (1986) *Home Is Where We Start From: Essays by a Psychoanalyst*. C. Winnicott (ed.). London: Penguin.

Chapter 9

Centre for Social Justice (2008) *Couldn't Care Less. A Policy Report from the Children in Care Working Group*. London: CSJ.

Children's Workforce Development Council (2008) *The state of the Childrens's Social Care Workforce 2008: Summary Report*. Leeds: CWDC.

Clay, D., Ludvigsen, A., Winchester, R. and Woolnough, R. (2008) *As Long as it Takes – A New Politics for Children*. 19th September. London: Action for Children.

Office of the High Commission for Human Rights (OHCHR) (2008) (49th session) *Report by Committee on the Rights of the Child*. (CRC/C/GBR/CO/4.) New York: OHCHR.

Piper, H. and Smith, (2003) '"Touch" in education and care settings: dilemmas and responses', *British Education Research Journal*, 29(6): 879–94.

Small, M.F. (2001) *Kids – How Biology and Culture Shape the Way We Raise Young Children*. New York: Anchor Books

Spall, B. and Callis, S. (1997) *Loss, Bereavement and Grief: A Guide to Effective Caring*. Cheltenham: Stanley Thornes.

United Nations Children's Fund (UNICEF) (2007) 'Child poverty in perspective: An overview of child well-being in rich countries', *Innocenti Report Card 7*. Florence: UNICEF Innocenti Research Centre.

Utting, W. (1997) *The Report of the Review of the Safeguards for Children Living Away from Home*. London: HMSO.

Zimbardo, P.G. (2007) *The Lucifer Effect: Understanding How Good People Turn Evil*. New York: Random House.

Index

Added to the page number, 'f' denotes a figure, 't' denotes a table and 'I' denotes an illustration.

emotional pain
  causes 67–8
  gaining insight 69
'emotionally harming' parenting 18
emotions
  language of 42
  theoretical constructions 39–40
empathy 17, 42, 43, 44
  and attuned relationships 14, 27
  effect on violence 14, 42
empowerment 32
  of staff 122
evaluation
  measurement and 105–8
  of the quality of services and organisations
    108–9
Every Child Matters 3, 17, 111
  links with the Pillars of Parenting 25t

F
family, role in anti-social behaviour 41, 44, 48, 50
fear-induced aggression 52
functionalist model of emotions 40

G
goal attainment scaling 108
'good parenting' 9, 21, 22, 43, 63
  curriculum for 21
government initiatives 3, 36, 50, 81, 132
    see also The Children's Plan; *Every Child
      Matters*
guilt 44

H
hard-edge problems for carers 64
high-achievers 5, 36, 77, 83
'Holding Safely' 63
hugs, giving and receiving 29, 125

I
'innate-plus-acquired' parenting skills'
    theory 1–2
insecure attachment 12–13, 14, 16, 84
instrumental aggression 52
inter-male aggression 52
international standards on treatment of
    children 125, 128
The Invention of Childhood 2

K
Kohlberg's theory of moral development 44

L
leadership
  difference between management and 119
  importance 114, 119–21
  parenting style as a practice model 120

learned aggression 52
life outcomes *see* outcomes
looked-after children *see* children in public care
The Lucifer Effect 130

M
management
  difference between leadership and 119
  responsibility of 118
  training 115
Managing Challenging Behaviour 83–4
Maslow's hierarchy of human needs
    25, 26f, 30, 32
maternal care, quality 13
measurement and evaluation 105–8
mental health, definition 90
mental health problems 48
  and emotional competence 41
  see also depression
moral conscience, development 44
moral context, placing behaviour 43
moral development, Kohlberg's theory 44
mortality rates, child 2
motivation, and sense of belonging 33–4
multi-disciplinary children's services 102, 104–5

N
National Care Standards for Scotland 121, 138–9
National Centre for Excellence in Residential
    Child Care 132
*National Minimum Standards and Regulations
    for Children's Homes* 9, 21–2, 26, 63
natural world, 'substitute carers' 2
needs
  of children 2, 26
  Maslow's hierarchy *see* Maslow's hierarchy
    of human needs
negative accommodation 76
neglect, abuse and *see* abuse and neglect
neuropsychological research 15–16, 28
NVQ Level 3 training 101, 111
  mismatch between practice skills and 6
  modifying 101–2

O
organisational capacity building 121
organisations
  bringing about change 120–1, 122
  evaluating 108–9
'organismic valuing theory' 77
orphanhood, effect on eminence and genius 77
outcomes
  and academic attainment 38, 79
  factors which make a difference 110, 113–14
  optimistic perspective 16
  and secure attachment 28
  see also poor outcomes; positive outcomes